40

Developing Executive Talent—a practical guide

Developing Executive Talent
a practical guide

Terry Farnsworth

London · New York · St Louis · San Francisco · Düsseldorf
Johannesburg · Kuala Lumpur · Mexico · Montreal · New Delhi
Panama · Paris · São Paulo · Singapore · Sydney · Toronto

Published by

McGRAW-HILL Book Company (UK) Limited
MAIDENHEAD· BERKSHIRE · ENGLAND

07 084457 7

Library of Congress Cataloging in Publication Data

Farnsworth, Terry.
    Developing executive talent.

    Bibliography: p.
    Includes index.
    1. Executives, Training of. 2. Executive ability. I. Title.
HF5549.5.T7F28   658.4'07   75-14495
ISBN 0-07-084457-7

10 9 8 7 6 5 4 3 2 1

Printed and bound in Great Britain.

Contents

Preface

This book is intended to fill a gap in the literature on executive development which perhaps reflects a weakness in management itself. After all, the task of developing an organization's human resources cannot simply be handed over to training specialists: it is an integral part of every manager's job.

The aim of this book is to provide practical guidance to all executives who wish to become more effective developers of people and to develop themselves through better self-management. It deals with those practical problems of training and self-development which all too often are glossed over in the literature and yet which frequently inhibit effective action.

It is quite unashamedly non-theoretical and down-to-earth and, I hope, virtually uncontaminated by training jargon. For far too long management training and development has been bedevilled by a surfeit of conflicting philosophies, instant panaceas and short-lived gimmicks. In this book I have tried to 'tell it as it is' and to provide practical solutions to real-life problems.

I hope that the book will be read by chief executives and directors as well as by line managers and training professionals and that all will find it worth the investment of their time. For me, training and development has always been a *business function* rather than a quasi-philanthropic activity which takes place exclusively in the classroom. I hope that this and other similar convictions will come through loud and clear.

Terry Farnsworth
January 1975

Foreword

The manager's job in the 'seventies is more difficult and challenging than it has ever been before. Reconciling statesmanlike vision and sensitivity with the gritty reality of making enough profit to survive tomorrow is not easy. And, by way of backcloth, there are turbulent economic and social changes, technological advances, new power relationships between politicians, unions and employers, and uncertainties in the supply and price of raw materials.

One encouragement is that companies are worried about how to deal with the problem of management development in practical terms, and no longer argue the case for and against it.

Terry Farnsworth's book makes three important contributions:

▶ It establishes the key point that, although there is no shortage of talent, imagination and drive, these qualities are trapped by antiquated structures and attitudes.

▶ It insists on the importance of personal self-development, rather than packages and programmes of universal application.

▶ It draws on the author's deep experience in explaining *how* to get on with the job and illustrates this with case material.

A book that should be read and used by all managers.

John Humble

Acknowledgements

My greatest debt is to the top management of 3M United Kingdom Limited for permitting many of the ideas and methods described in this book to be tried out within the Company. This applies particularly to Peter Hutchings, Director of Personnel and Industrial Relations, and to the two Managing Directors with whom I have worked, Jack Zoethout, the current MD, and Lee Gehrke, now Vice-President of Finance in the parent company in St Paul, Minnesota.

Outside 3M, I am especially grateful to Lyndon Jones, Principal of South-West London College, but for whose encouragement this book would probably not have been written. Further back in my career I owe a great deal to men like Tom Wheeldon and Tony Mead of OTMA Limited, both of whom I regard as outstanding training professionals.

A few of the chapters in this book include material which has appeared in *Management Today* and *Industrial and Commercial Training* and I am most grateful to the respective Editors, Robert Heller and John Wellens, for their permission to make use of it here.

Part 1

What every chief executive and director should know

1
How to avoid some common pitfalls

The current boom in management development has produced a situation reminiscent of the early days of the Klondyke gold rush. New techniques, like new settlements, mushroom everywhere; dedicated professionals jostle for attention with smooth-talking men; rumours abound of discoveries which will enrich both companies and managers; substantial sums are gambled—and lost—upon prospectuses which, in some cases, turn out to be little short of fraudulent.

Yet despite the tumult and the euphoria, one thing is certain: management development is one of the least advanced, least understood and least validated of all management activities. It is still in its lusty, bawling infancy—inevitably so, since we have no proven theory of how managers learn. Nor do we know with certainty what motivates a manager to change his attitudes—why some are as eager to experiment as they are zestful in performance, while others show few signs of intellectual curiosity throughout their careers. Studies of managerial performance, based upon differences in age, education and social background, have produced many hypotheses, and even more generalizations, but a total lack of scientific laws. Much more is hidden than is known. It therefore behoves both the apostle and the practitioner of management development to speak softly and to carry a small stick.

Nevertheless, while management development, in evolutionary terms, is still in the Middle Ages, there is sufficient evidence to suggest that there are a number of attitudes and beliefs, commonly found in industry, which can distort and ultimately destroy any potential it may have for improving executive performance. I have classified this assembly of untruths and half-truths as 'myths', but no one should underestimate their continuing influence upon managerial thought and action—especially, unhappily, at board level where their influence upon company policy can be, and often is, quite lethal.

Five of these myths are particularly dangerous and worthy of analysis and comment.

3

Myth number 1: Desert island

Few directors would dispute that management development, if it is to be effective, must be fully integrated with the needs of the business. Yet, in many organizations, the management development function operates in a virtually watertight compartment within the general personnel department. It is almost wholly concerned with the organization and administration of training courses for managers and supervisors. Occasionally there are half-hearted attempts to provide other services such as counselling and career planning, but these are kept strictly subsidiary to the main purpose, which is to fill—and keep on filling—the maximum number of places at the company training centre. Terms such as 'throughput' and 'down time' abound in such departments and reports are proudly submitted at regular intervals, showing that x managers attended y courses during z period.

In essence, this is the factory-farming approach to management development. Managers are received in the requisite batches, are given the prescribed inoculations of management theory and are then 'processed' smoothly back to their units, leaving the training staff behind on their 'desert island' to await the next consignment of managerial course-fodder. It represents a completely vain attempt to apply the methods of production control to the infinitely more subtle problems of influencing human attitudes and behaviour, and is responsible for much of the cynicism which surrounds management development in many larger organizations.

However smoothly and efficiently such training centres may appear to be operating, however ancient their timbers or modern their facilities, boards would do well to ponder whether their activities are—or indeed ever can be—truly effective.

Myth number 2: Cap and gown

In spite of the current emphasis upon participative methods in management education, some directors continue to believe in the supposedly magical effects of the inspirational talk or lecture (upon their subordinates, not themselves). Sales directors are particularly vulnerable to this myth since many believe, albeit surreptitiously, that selling essentially involves a trial of strength between personalities rather than a joint satisfaction of mutual needs. The truth is that no man can be taught anything, even by the most gifted speaker, unless he is *willing* to learn and can see that by doing so he will achieve his own personal goals. He may applaud the speaker's virtuosity, just as he might applaud the performance of a favourite singer or comedian on television. But the lasting effect upon his performance as a manager will be no greater than that of the television programme upon his ability to sing or tell jokes.

Lecturing, as Voltaire pointed out two centuries ago, is a form of attack, and even the most polished performer may fail to penetrate the inner citadel of a manager's beliefs and values—the very factors which exert the strongest influence upon his job performance. Moreover, since such 'cap and gown' methods have been virtually abandoned in the teaching of infants, why should they be thought appropriate to the needs of experienced managers? Much is still unknown about the learning process, especially as it applies to the practising manager, but one thing is clear: little that is new will be retained unless it is *discovered* by the man himself—unless it clarifies or codifies his experience, or provides him with a new vantage-point from which to reassess his existing judgements and opinions.

Directors should therefore be wary of placing too much trust in oratorical princes, however dazzling their rhetoric or powerful their personalities. Like a pain-killing injection, their effect is only temporary. When the euphoria is over and the last verbal fusillades have been fired, the responsibility for initiating change will remain where it has always been—with the board, the chief executive and the managers themselves.

Myth number 3: Panacea

During the Middle Ages, much time and energy were expended upon a fruitless search for the philosopher's stone, a mythical base metal which, it was hoped, would provide a cheap and endless supply of gold. In much the same way, the history of management development is littered with the wreckage of ill-fated attempts to produce a magical elixir which would instantly transform a manager's performance and enable him to scale new heights of effectiveness in his job. There have been T-Groups and Grid Plans, case studies and business games, job enrichment and job enlargement, Theory X and Theory Y, psycho-cybernetics and transactional analysis—every year the list grows longer and more confusing. Each of these nostrums has its merits; each may be relevant to particular types of management problem. And yet, almost without exception, all have been over-sold by their devotees, with a notable disregard for intellectual humility and, in some cases, common sense.

None—not even those which have been widely implemented—have brought about a managerial millennium. And not surprisingly, since neither the job of managing nor the manager himself can be reduced to the level of a Pavlovian experiment: conditioned reflexes, like patriotism, are not enough. The scepticism displayed by many experienced managers towards the claims of the pedlars of managerial wonder-drugs is rooted not (as is so often stated) in an aversion to change but in an intuitive suspicion that, lurking beneath the sonorous phraseology, there is generally a profound over-simplification of the problems which real-life executives have to face.

Another contributory factor is the speed at which fashions seem to change in this area; the 'authorities' of today all too quickly become the outcasts of

5

tomorrow. For example, until fairly recently, the beliefs of the environmental school of industrial psychologists (the so-called 'heating and ventilation men') were held just as fiercely—and trumpeted just as loudly—as those of the modern 'behavioural scientist'. Yet how much of the old order remains today? And what assurance can there be that the theories of the newcomers will not also eventually prove to have been built on shifting sands? The answer, of course, is none. This does *not* mean that directors and managers should be inherently contemptuous of new concepts and techniques: it *does* mean that the theoreticians would do well to adopt attitudes which are somewhat less oracular and messianic. It is no accident that the term 'scientific management' is now used far less frequently than in the heady days of Taylor and Fayol—nor that no one has yet had the temerity to write a book entitled *The* Laws *of Modern Management*. Directors, managers and theorists alike, we are all students now.

Myth number 4: Black magic

If management development experts were to dress in accordance with the expectations which they frequently arouse during boardroom discussions, there would be a thriving domestic market for the manufacturers of leopard-skin cloaks and tribal head-dresses. Particularly in those companies in which he constitutes a new species of executive, the management development specialist is sometimes regarded as a kind of industrial witch-doctor whose spells and incantations can cause even the most withered managerial plants to blossom and prosper.

However, as was pointed out earlier in this chapter, no manager can be developed, as it were, by artificial insemination: he needs an incentive to learn—one which makes sense in terms of his own personal beliefs and aspirations. Every management developer knows that a lively performance in the classroom carries no guarantee that a man will apply his knowledge when he returns to his job. And yet it is the job situation, with all its built-in pressures and challenges, which provides the main seed-bed for a manager's development; by comparison, the influence of formal classroom teaching is of relatively minor significance. Another primary factor in the development process is the calibre of the man's immediate superior, especially his ability as a 'coach', i.e., whether he can succeed in passing on his knowledge and experience in such a way that the subordinate will be constantly 'stretching' to meet high standards of performance.

It is totally unrealistic to expect the management development specialist to work miracles when the two most important factors in the situation are beyond his control: this is why management development is, and can only be, a line management responsibility. As in other functions of the business, the role of the specialist is supportive, not executive.

Alistair Mant,* in his report on management development for the British Institute of Management, pointed out that an effective organization structure and a sensible reward system are often more effective in improving managerial performance than formal management development programmes. Such matters are clearly a board responsibility. A similar harvest may be reaped from systematic selection and promotion policies since, unless men of the right calibre are selected for management jobs, they can hardly be expected to develop their subordinates. And yet, in practice, the ability to 'grow' subordinates is rarely regarded—or even recognized—as an important yardstick of a manager's effectiveness: hence the continual succession problems encountered by many companies when key managers resign or retire.

For executives at any level to regard the management development specialist as the possessor of almost magical powers of inspiration is to deny both their own responsibilities and the realities of business life. And, flattering though it may be to him to be so regarded, the management development man would do well to reflect that, even in primitive societies, the job of the witch-doctor is notoriously insecure.

Myth number 5: Slide rule

Management development is primarily concerned with changing attitudes and only marginally with the acquisition of knowledge and skills. And rightly so, since attitudes condition performance and results: in the absence of the will to apply it, knowledge, by itself, is impotent. But changes in attitudes are not merely difficult to measure; there is often a noticeable discrepancy between what a manager professes to believe (for example, after his exposure to new ideas on a training course) and how he, in fact, behaves when he returns to the job. Even improvements in his performance can rarely be attributed solely to the influence of the course. There are a host of other factors which, either singly or in combination, can exert a more decisive influence.

It follows that attempts to measure the precise benefits of management development—the so called 'slide rule' approach—are essentially futile and misconceived. One can no more hope to measure such benefits than one can the human states of happiness or sorrow, since in each case there are far too many contributing factors which defy quantification. And yet this search for 'measurement' produces much noisy breast-beating—and even more pointless 'research'—among management development specialists, many of whom, perhaps understandably, would feel more confident if they were able to show a causal relationship between their own efforts and the subsequent performance of their managerial 'pupils'.

Let directors beware. No such relationship has been found to exist, nor is it ever likely to while managers continue to exercise their human freedom to

* *The experienced manager: a major resource*, BIM Books, 1970.

succeed or fail. And the management development specialist who cannot live with the 'frustration' of not being able to quantify his results would do better to emigrate to the more agreeable pastures of accountancy or work study (though, even there, he would encounter some surprises). The most that any training man can do is to ensure that his objectives and methods are relevant to the situation and that his personal skills, as consultant, salesman and teacher, are of a high order. After that, his responsibility ends—while that of the board, for managing the business, continues unabated.

In conclusion, I must stress that it is not my intention to 'debunk' management development—far from it—but to draw attention to the fact that, as a relatively new and emerging specialization, too much should not be expected of it by directors at so early a stage in its development. It is no substitute for effective business management, nor can it transform chronically poor performers into swashbuckling entrepreneurs. At present, we know far more about its limitations than its effectiveness. Only one thing is certain: that we must have the courage to persevere.

2

How to establish a management development policy

A progressive organization, particularly if it is expanding, finds itself utterly obliged to spend time and money on management development. Among other reasons, if it does not do so, it is unlikely either to retain its most able people or to attract men of high potential. In today's increasingly competitive conditions, management development is no longer a luxury, the plaything of a few indulgent industrial titans. It is a necessity for survival and a prerequisite for growth.

But what *is* management development and what are its rightful concerns? How can a company establish a soundly-based development programme which embodies businesslike philosophies and attitudes? Is it merely a question of providing a conveyor belt of training courses, both internal and external—the so-called factory farming approach? Or is it an altogether more subtle and complex process in which courses and seminars form only the tip of the development iceberg, while the real action, as always, takes place in the gruelling arena of the job, with all its built-in challenges and opportunities? These are the questions which this chapter seeks to answer.

Firstly, let us quickly dispel one lingering illusion about management development: that it is just another specialist function, which can safely be left in the hands of erudite theoreticians with the gift of unlocking the secrets of human motivation. Management development is broad, not narrow, in scope; it is the concern of all managers, not a closed shop to all but a selected few. Just as a firm's marketing effort supplies the spearhead of its struggle for survival, so the task of management development is to ensure that the attack is pressed home by troops who know their job, have faith in their weapons and commanders, and whose morale is a reflection of their confidence in their own professionalism. In short, management development refers to any aspect of a man's employment which causes him to expand his inherent capabilities and thereby increase his usefulness to the business. Traditionally, it deals with such questions as:

How can men's knowledge, skills and attitudes be improved?
What motivates a person to develop within an organization?
What methods of education and training are appropriate to various skills; and to various people?

But this is only a beginning. Management development is really an aspect of *management planning* which, in turn, is the process of analysing the current and future management needs of the company in relation to its economic plans and of ensuring an adequate supply of trained personnel. This requirement instantly raises such further questions as:

What kind of arrangements should be made for succession?
How far should managers be responsible for developing potential successors?
What information is needed to ensure that managerial transfers and promotions are carried out equitably and effectively?

Even now the picture is still not complete. Management development also has important implications for *organization structure*, since an individual's development, or the lack of it, may well precipitate the need for changes in the structure in order to accommodate the best distribution of abilities. It cannot be divorced from such problems as:

Which is the best kind of organization structure for a particular activity?
How are objectives for managers to be set and agreed?
What review techniques and safeguards should be introduced in appraising performance?

Clearly, the answers to questions of this magnitude cannot be the sole prerogative of specialists, important though their contribution may be. They can be answered authoritatively only by those who are responsible for the general direction and control of the enterprise as a whole. In other words, management development, if it is to be effective, requires a firm bedrock of policy, i.e., written statements, couched in broad terms, of the objectives and courses of action intended by the company in the fulfilment of its purpose. Without such a foundation, development activities will quickly become arbitrary and unintegrated.

How can such a policy be established and what are the principles upon which it should be based? In my view there are three working assumptions which constitute the essential starting points for an effective approach to management development.

1. **The training and development of managers must be integrated with company objectives**—Training programmes and development activities must be planned

10

to meet specific company objectives and be based on a careful analysis of the needs of both groups and individuals.

2. Managers are the best developers of their subordinates—They have immediate contact with them at all times and are in the best position to coach and to counsel them. This does *not* mean that a manager must undertake personally all the activities that may be necessary to develop his subordinates. It *does* mean that he is accountable for ensuring that they are provided with the opportunities, both on and off the job, which are necessary for their development.

3. The job itself offers the best opportunities for development—Nothing is more effective in growing managers than a challenging job that stretches an individual's abilities and provides him with opportunities to demonstrate his potential. All off-the-job activities, such as courses and seminars, should be aimed at improving a manager's effectiveness in his present job or at preparing him for a position of greater complexity and responsibility which he might attain in the foreseeable future.

My own company is fortunate in that the main condition for the success of management development activities, top management's own involvement in them, has long since been fulfilled. For example, during the past year, the managing director has taken a leading role in organizing the training of senior management in advanced marketing techniques and has participated in business management exercises which bring together managers from all sectors of the company. Given such a setting of support and encouragement, there is every prospect of success for the variety of other development techniques which we use. Without it, there is little doubt that they would be an almost complete waste of time and money.

Let us now consider how these 'working assumptions' can be woven into a written statement of company policy on management development. The example which I have chosen is derived from a consultancy assignment which I carried out in a medium-sized company with a conventional line and staff organization structure, consisting of virtually autonomous manufacturing divisions and a small number of advisory staff groups. I have set out below some of the principal provisions of the Management Development Policy Statement, together with brief comments designed to clarify and expand the underlying principles upon which they are based. Like all policy documents, it simply represents a declaration of the company's intentions: the responsibility for implementing the policy rests with managers at all levels in the company.

▶ Each division and staff group is responsible for initiating the development activities necessary to provide the company with the quantity and quality of management required to achieve its objectives. This means

11

being adequately prepared to provide replacements due to promotions, transfers, retirements or terminations of managers at any level.

The key word here is 'adequately'. Clearly, no manager can fully anticipate all his needs, e.g., losses arising from death. 'Adequately' implies that managers will anticipate their manpower needs as much as possible and avoid the kind of crisis which can so easily arise when there is a need to replace a key man.

▶ In addition to the present two-yearly Management Audit, each division and group will review periodically both the quantity and quality of its management to determine whether it is adequate to meet established objectives, both for the present and the future. Such reviews will highlight the specific development activities which need to be undertaken.

The requirement here is that each major operation will keep its manpower under constant review in order to identify specific individual development needs and to provide a basis for group development plans. Without such periodic reviews (normally every six months) development activities run the risk of becoming irrelevant to the real needs.

▶ Development activities will be aimed at meeting specific development needs arising from a manager's performance in his present job or those anticipated in future assignments of greater complexity and responsibility.

Underlines the fact that 90 per cent of a manager's development takes place on the job and that development activities which are job-oriented are likely to have the greater impact upon his performance.

▶ Communications and coordination between divisions and groups, and between managers at all levels, must be such that a climate is created in which maximum opportunities occur for management development.

Stresses a manager's responsibility for maintaining effective three-way communications and for fostering team effort with other departments. He must actively seek information which would be helpful to his own development and to the development of his subordinates.

▶ All development activities will be continuously audited to determine their effectiveness in providing the necessary quantity and quality of management to meet the company's present and future objectives.

Points to the need for the regular monitoring of development activities to prevent them from becoming irrelevant or obsolete. Highlights the need for continuous feedback to evaluate their effectiveness—a factor which is frequently overlooked in management development programmes.

▶ The personnel staff group will provide functional assistance to all divisions and groups in the planning, conducting and auditing of management development activities at all levels.

Reminds managers that while they remain accountable for the development of their subordinates, they can call upon specialist assistance at any time— and are encouraged to do so.

Policies must be communicated effectively if they are to fulfil their rightful function of providing the guidelines within which managers can act. And in so sensitive an area as management development, with all its inherent implications for the achievement of a manager's personal goals and ambitions, such policies must be *written*. It is all too easy for a company to defer the kind of commitment which written policies involve by raising the twin spectres of bureaucracy and rigidity as excuses for relying upon unwritten codes of practice which can be conveniently interpreted, however inconsistently, as a means of avoiding or dealing with embarrassing situations. This is a distinctly short-sighted approach; one which is certain, in the long run, to raise grave doubts among managers about the capacity, the sincerity, and even the integrity, of top management. For, to quote Abraham Lincoln, one cannot hope to *fool all of the people all of the time*, least of all in an area of personnel policy which touches so closely upon every manager's career prospects and personal aspirations.

But merely to produce written policies is not enough. All too often they disappear into a manager's administrative manual where, after a cursory reading, they quickly attain the status of historical documents which have little effect in conditioning his thinking in decision-making situations. Having formulated a management development policy, top management must make every effort to ensure that it is sold to all concerned. There are certain obvious and traditional methods which can be used—articles in the house journal, announcements on notice boards, management circulars and memoranda and specially-convened meetings at which a member of the board, often the managing director himself, explains the thinking behind the policy and the objectives which it is designed to achieve.

But there are other and more imaginative techniques which can be employed to good effect. For example, my own company and many other organizations have wide-ranging programmes of internal management training courses, providing admirable opportunities for the dissemination and discussion of management development policy. The familiar contents of such courses—subjects such as planning, delegation, motivation and performance appraisal—give excellent opportunities for the firm's policy to be examined in the light of the best current thinking and practice. Assuming that it has been well thought out and clearly written, there is a worthwhile motivational plus to be gained from encouraging frank discussion of a policy in the context of a course concerned with improving management performance. Many a chip can be removed

13

from many a managerial shoulder in such circumstances; many misconceptions and half-truths can be authoritatively exposed and remedied.

There is much discussion today in both academic and management circles on the mechanics of policy formulation, especially in the area of personnel policy which affects all employees, regardless of function. Should policy be formulated democratically by the many or autocratically by the few? Should it reflect a consensus of managerial opinion or simply represent the best judgement of those with the most relevant knowledge and experience? It may well be that those current developments in our society towards greater participation in decision-making, which are affecting so many of our established institutions, will one day play a more aggressive role at the grass-roots level of policy planning, especially in such areas as management development, salary administration and internal promotion systems. Be that as it may, there is no indication at present that such a revolution is imminent, nor is it likely to become an issue in those companies in which both the formal and the informal communications networks are already operating effectively, providing the kind of feedback that prevents policies from becoming irrelevant or obsolete.

Once again, lively discussions on management development policy during internal training courses, together with other relevant data from career planning interviews and counselling sessions, if reported promptly, can do much to ensure that the higher echelons become quickly aware of any cracks which may be developing in the policy edifice. The management development officer forms the logical communications channel through which these grass-roots opinions and attitudes can be transmitted to top management. (He should not be expected to reveal the identities of the managers whose views he may express.)

In this chapter, I have stressed the importance of establishing a coherent statement of policy as a prerequisite of effective development efforts. In recent years many companies have established a management development function for the first time and are understandably anxious to obtain quick results. Such companies are tempted to hurl themselves into a maelstrom of activities in an effort to prove, to themselves and to others, that at last something is happening—something from which it is believed, with all the fervour of the newly-converted, only good can result. When these efforts, unplanned and uncoordinated as they so often are, prove counterproductive, disillusion and despair spread like a virus throughout the ranks of management. The brave new world collapses amid a chorus of cynicism, back-biting and mutual recrimination.

Formulating a policy for management development, as for other key areas of business activity, is not simply a barren intellectual exercise: it is a prime requirement for effective results, as necessary to the achievement of objectives as is a compass to the master of a ship. To be sure, a vessel can be operated without a compass but not without the grossest misuse of resources, nor with-

14

out exposing the crew to unnecessary hazards. Practical businessmen think through their policies first: actions come later. They know, too well, the bitter truth underlying Stephen Leacock's celebrated quip: 'Having lost sight of our objectives, we redoubled our efforts.'

3

How to use external courses

In theory at least, sending a manager on an external training course is no different from any other business investment. Just as a firm may decide to plough back part of its profits into new plant and machinery, so too it may resolve to invest in a manager whose future potential seems bright with promise. And yet all too often the money spent on such courses is utterly wasted, resulting in massive frustration for both the company and the individual. Frequently the wrong men are sent on the wrong courses for the wrong reasons and at the wrong time. How can such disasters be avoided? Here are eight basic ground rules for companies wishing to obtain a worthwhile return:

1. **Always have a clear business objective.** Do not send a manager on a course because management training is 'fashionable' or because it seems a good way of rewarding him for long and faithful service. To send a moderate performer on a sophisticated management programme is not merely wasteful—it is downright cruel. Surrounded by higher calibre men who will quickly regard him as a 'lame duck' and bombarded with advanced theories which are well beyond his mental reach, he is likely to return with his self-confidence undermined.

There are only two valid reasons for sending a man on a course: his need to improve his performance in his current job (and the company's belief that he has the capacity to do so); or to equip him with knowledge and skills which he will need in a job which he is due to take over—hopefully, in the reasonably near future. In other words, send him because his mind needs to be stretched and because there is evidence which suggests that he is *capable* of being stretched. For unless he has the capacity to grow, the course will only heighten his sense of inadequacy and his subsequent performance may well deteriorate.

2. **Make sure that he wants to go.** The one excuse which should always be disregarded is that grand old favourite 'pressure of work'. Of course, a good manager is always busy: this is presumably why he remains on the payroll. But there is never likely to be a time when he is not busy: and indeed the fact that he is hard-pressed may be one of the best possible reasons for sending the manager away for a mental spring-clean.

However, it is quite a different matter when a man protests, sincerely and maybe even aggressively, that he is simply not interested in attending a course. Whether we like it or not, some managers just do not believe in management education and, if sent against their wishes, will often react by playing a disruptive role throughout the whole of the course. In extreme cases, such men can virtually wreck a course with their continual cynicism and general intransigence. A man who does not want to be educated, or believes that he cannot be, is no candidate for a management development programme. A mule, no less than a horse, cannot be made to drink.

3. **Do not try to change his personality.** Some psychologists believe that an individual's basic personality pattern is fixed by the age of five (indeed, a few claim that it is fixed during the first six months of life). Be that as it may, it is the height of *naïveté* to believe that a manager of mature years with deeply entrenched views on human behaviour, based upon his own interpretation of what 'life' has taught him, can be changed in any radical way by a few days' exposure to the latest behavioural science theories. It is just not on.

True, there may be some slight broadening of his views or softening of his prejudices. But as the course recedes into the distance he is likely to revert to type and to practise the 'truths' which he really believes in rather than those to which he has paid lip-service in the classroom. Usually the best that can be hoped for is that he will become more aware of the impact of his behaviour upon others: but such an awareness does not necessarily lead to permanent change.

The time to assess the real effect of these courses is not (as so often happens) during the first few weeks after the man's return, but after at least six months have elapsed, or even a year. In most cases it will be found that such changes as have occurred have been peripheral at best. Depressing as it may seem, this is hardly surprising. After all, managers are not robots.

4. **Ensure that he is properly briefed.** Many managers are thrust into management training programmes without a word of explanation as to why they were selected, what the course is about and how it is hoped that they will benefit in the future. Few companies realize just how worrying it can be for a manager to find himself in a totally new environment surrounded by strangers and uncertain whether he will be able to cope with the demands which will be made upon him. Indeed it may be several days before he 'unfreezes' sufficiently to take in the course material. Since many of the longer courses involve a heavy work-load of lectures, discussions and planned reading, he may fall behind and become depressed.

17

Such problems and difficulties can be avoided completely if the manager is adequately briefed well in advance of his attendance at the course. Explain to him that he is going to find new and different solutions to problems he has been used to meeting, but that this does not necessarily mean that he has been wrong in his approach. Give him time to get adjusted to the fact that he is going on the course and to make plans for the work of his department to be reorganized during his absence.

Tell him that he is not expected to run his operation by remote control while he is away and to instruct his secretary to contact him only in circumstances of extreme urgency. Inform him that he can serve his own and the company's interest best by concentrating wholeheartedly upon the course and keeping a sharp look-out for any useful ideas. Without undue flattery, it should also be made clear to him that he has been selected because his judgement is respected and that his reactions to the course may well determine whether other managers at his level will attend in the future.

To summarize, a manager who is well briefed is likely to be far more positive in his attitudes than one who has simply been thrown in at the deep end. No modern general would expect his troops to carry out a successful assault without a proper briefing. Why should we expect managers to behave any differently?

5. Vet the course carefully. There are more than 800 training organizations currently operating in the UK, each claiming to have expertise in various aspects of management training. To select a course purely on the basis of the blurb in the course leaflet is about as intelligent as booking one's holiday at the resort with the glossiest brochure. And yet given the veritable monsoon of course literature which rains down upon companies with practically every post, how is it possible to separate the professionals from the charlatans?

It helps considerably if a firm has friendly contacts with other companies which have used a particular course—even though such informal vetting is far from foolproof. Unquestionably the surest and safest method of checking a course, however, is to use the professional services which are available through the Management Courses Index and the British Institute of Management. Both of these organizations carry extensive reports on a wide variety of management training courses, and their assessments, either by telephone or in writing, are readily available to member-organizations. Considering the heavy expense involved in sending a manager on all but the shortest management courses, membership of these bodies offers an extremely worthwhile insurance policy against the kind of catastrophe which occurs when the course is 'a shot in the dark'.

Incidentally, any company using external courses should begin to build up its own internal records by requiring managers to submit short written reports on the courses which they have attended. Such reports are perhaps even more valuable than the MCI and BIM evaluations in that they represent the assessments of men who are totally familiar with the company's environment and are thus well placed to judge the course.

6. Make sure that the course is participative. Managers, especially senior managers, resent being constantly talked at; they like to do plenty of talking themselves and to share their experiences with others. This is exactly as it should be. Successful and experienced senior executives can hardly be expected to listen interminably to a course leader whose practical experience of management may be considerably less than their own. This is not to denigrate course leaders; they frequently have special skills in communicating and discussion-leading which enable them to be invaluable catalysts and chairmen.

Nevertheless, any management course which does not allow for a high degree of participation by the course members is doomed to failure. As practical men facing practical problems, the vast majority of managers are interested in theory only to the extent that it unlocks doors to workable solutions. This is a lesson which some management educationalists have still to absorb, and yet it is absolutely fundamental to the manager's learning process. Whether the course deals with general management problems or with specific functional techniques, it is vital that the course members have ample opportunities to apply what they have learned to situations and problems which are as close to real life as is possible in practice. This means a minimum of lecturing and a much greater emphasis upon group discussion, case studies, business games and various forms of role-playing. After all, it is better for a manager to have fought only mock-battles during a course than never to have fought at all.

7. Avoid 'holiday camps'. There are still far too many management courses which do not offer a sufficient challenge to the course members. Invariably, such programmes are held in elegant country houses in close proximity to first-class golf courses or in luxurious hotels, complete with swimming pools and sauna baths and television in every room. While no one suggests that managers who attend external courses should wear hair shirts or live a life of monastic simplicity, neither is it necessary to distract them from their endeavours by the too-flamboyant trappings of the *dolce vita*.

If the accommodation is comfortable, the food good and the conference room pleasant and well ventilated, there is no need whatever for the course to be held amid surroundings of Byzantine splendour. The delegates have a job of work to do and cannot be expected to buckle down to the course if the extramural attractions of the conference venue are constantly uppermost in their minds. Indeed, one suspects that some organizations use such attractions as inducements for managers to attend their courses ('you may not learn anything, old boy, but your handicap will improve').

Such a policy is utterly self-defeating. Course members cannot be expected to participate enthusiastically if they are half asleep after a night on the town.

The time for such revelries is on the last night of the course, when the battle is over.

8. Be prepared to follow up. A manager who returns from a course anxious to practise a new technique or skill will quickly lose his enthusiasm if his efforts are met with hostility or indifference. Frankly, it is a complete waste of time and money for a company to send a manager on a course and yet to frustrate his every attempt to use his new-found knowledge. To do so is simply to build in frustration and to encourage him to leave such a 'reactionary' concern. The lesson is clear. When a company sends a man to a training programme for change and development, it must in a figurative way say to itself, 'I will change and develop and grow too'.

The make-or-break factor in this delicate post-course period is the attitude of the man's immediate boss. If he is sympathetic and supportive, patient and tolerant, the chances are that the manager will more than justify his attendance by his improved performance. But if the boss is negative or carping and ever ready to scoff at 'new-fangled theories' then the man's performance, instead of improving, may well deteriorate to a point far below his pre-course standard.

Finally, since there are so many pitfalls involved in sending a manager on an external course, the question arises: 'is it worth the risk?' The answer is a resounding 'yes'—provided that the company takes a businesslike approach to its investment and carries out the kind of research which has been suggested in this chapter. Naturally, even with the most careful vetting, there will still be occasional failures. But this in no way justifies a company in cutting itself off from the outside world, with all the attendant dangers of complacency and inbreeding. Given sensible pre-course planning and realistic expectations, most managers will come away from a professionally-run development activity wiser men than when they went into it. The fact that perfection can rarely be achieved is no reason for ceasing to aspire to it. That way lies stagnation and ultimate decay.

4

How and how not to appraise managers

In every working relationship it is necessary for a manager to appraise the performance of his subordinates—otherwise there would be no rationale for his decisions about differential rewards. And yet the history of appraisal systems is one of confrontation and conflict, of poisoned relationships and frustrated hopes. Indeed, as every personnel manager knows, disagreements about performance are a major factor in executive turnover and even when a man does not leave he is frequently embittered by his experiences. Similarly, the judgements which are made during the processes of external recruitment and selection are equally vulnerable to error and miscalculation and can have a serious effect upon the company's performance.

The question arises: what tools and methods are used by companies to assess the performance of their human resources? How effective are they? What are their strengths and limitations and does a study of their various track records hold out any greater promise for the future? Stripped of the mystique which often surrounds them, most of these techniques can be grouped into six main types.

1. **The intuitive approach.** This is the most primitive and yet the most enduring form of appraisal. It has nothing to do with facts or with rational assessment: it is purely a matter of 'gut reaction' to another person's chemistry, of good or bad 'vibrations', inexplicable yet real. The selection interview is the great happy hunting-ground of this type of appraiser, the kind of man who claims to be able to assess a candidate 'as he comes through the door'. For such an interviewer the die is cast virtually before a word has been spoken and he spends most of his time searching for evidence, however spurious, which he can use to give his prejudices a veneer of objectivity.

The longer that such a man stays in a professional recruitment role, the more likely it is that these prejudices will harden and eventually ossify. This is one of the reasons why so many large companies are staffed by executives of precisely the same type, so that sooner or later the organization begins to falter from lack of creative oxygen. Indeed, in a company where the majority of managers think alike, dress alike and sometimes even look alike, it is most unlikely that radical new thinking will ever take root. The result is that when the company succumbs to a take-over or merger there invariably follows a traumatic period of house-cleaning during which the so-called 'dead wood' is consigned to the scrap-heap.

Whether it is used in recruitment or in the evaluation of performance, the intuitive method is the arch-enemy of originality and innovation—indeed of any type of behaviour which does not fit the existing corporate mould. Those executives who begin to express their individualism are quickly made aware that they must adapt or perish. Many a promising executive has resigned because he has been told by his superior 'sorry, old boy, but you are just not our type'.

2. Personality-centred appraisal. One of the late Douglas McGregor's strongest convictions was that managers object to 'playing God'. Nevertheless, judging from the number of appraisal schemes which require the assessment of an individual's personality traits, one might be forgiven for supposing that they positively revel in such a role. Indeed, when a manager is given such qualities to assess as 'honesty', 'trustworthiness', 'dependability' and 'maturity', it is well-nigh impossible for him to avoid assuming the role of the amateur psychiatrist. And, not surprisingly, he often interprets such questions as meaning simply, 'Do I like him?'.

During the past decade the 'trait approach' has fallen into disfavour with management theorists but there is little doubt that it continues to exert a powerful influence upon managerial decision-making. For example, the executive appointment columns still reverberate to clarion-calls for 'men of enthusiasm and initiative'. 'Drive' is another quality which is frequently mentioned (one wonders just how many applicants would consider themselves deficient in this respect). The truth is, of course, that such qualities do not lend themselves to objective measurement. They are simply a function of a man's natural ability and of the many other factors in the job situation which either help or hinder him from fulfilling his potential. Managers who persist in believing that they can assess such traits are not merely deluding themselves: they are unwittingly revealing their own immaturity and lack of perception.

But still it goes on, this fruitless search for the 'ideal personality', aided and abetted by those plausible pedlars of esoteric tests who claim to be able to unlock the secrets of an executive's psyche. Once again, this is simply a recipe for organizational inertia. All that happens, as with the intuitive method, is that those who survive the tests are virtually indistinguishable from each other in temperament and outlook. They merely strengthen the myopia of that self-perpetuating oligarchy of senior managers, which all too often results in the downfall of the company.

22

3. Group selection. This is an extremely attractive form of appraisal which is used both for recruitment and internal promotion purposes—and increasingly (as in 3M UK) for defining training needs. Attractive because, unlike some of the more conventional methods, it enables judgements to be made on the basis of a candidate's actual performance during a number of practical exercises which are carefully structured to expose his strengths and weaknesses. Essentially it represents a Darwinian approach to the problems of appraisal—'let's throw them in at the deep end and see who can swim'.

The trouble with this method is that it is frequently used as a make-or-break factor in the selection process instead of being regarded merely as another input. All is staked upon one throw of the dice, regardless of the fact that a candidate may be below par, both mentally and physically, during the period of the exercises. For example, a man who has barely recovered from a bout of influenza or who is undergoing difficulties in his personal life can hardly be expected to be at his best. Another grave drawback of this type of appraisal is that it is biased in favour of those candidates who are natural extroverts and who are not overawed by the presence of senior managers acting as assessors. In the final analysis, however, the method stands or falls by the quality of the assessors' judgements and their willingness to tolerate views and opinions which may be very different from their own. Judging by the criticisms which continue to be levelled at civil service and officer selection boards, the inherent tendency of such boards to select from a somewhat narrow range of human types constitutes a danger which has yet to be fully overcome.

The group selection method has been derided by its critics as 'the con man's paradise' but, so long as its limitations are recognized, it can provide valuable additional data about a man—especially on how he interacts with other members of the group. It is most effective in identifying men who are likely to succeed in jobs where the ability to communicate is the vital ingredient, e.g., salesmen, sales managers and training specialists—or in identifying the training needs of men who are already in such jobs. Conversely, it is least successful when used to select for jobs requiring a high level of creativity and analytical thinking.

4. Written reports. While middle and junior levels of management are generally covered by more standardized appraisal procedures, the performance of senior executives is frequently the subject of confidential written reports. This practice is based upon the premise that, since higher-level managers enjoy a greater freedom to 'grow' their jobs, they ought not to be appraised against the same yardsticks as more routine workers. Inevitably, in those companies which use such reports, they are regarded by executives as a status symbol.

The fatal flaw in most written reporting systems is that they assume the presence of a talent which is all too rare in management: the ability to write clear, perceptive, analytical prose. The result is that many reports are so woolly and vague as to be virtually useless for appraisal purposes. Again, the absence of specific performance criteria opens the floodgates to the amateur psychiatrist and many a distorted 'profile' has been drawn through a subtle combination of incompetence and malice. This, in turn, raises another issue which is common to all appraisal systems: the problem of feedback of information to the individual who has been appraised. But whereas the majority of conventional appraisal systems require the appraiser to discuss his comments with his subordinate at a personal interview, this happens far less frequently in the case of written reports. Moreover, even when such a discussion is held, it is only rarely that the executive is allowed to read his report. He is therefore entirely dependent upon his superior's ability and willingness to reflect the true tone of the report, as opposed to merely commenting upon those items which are least likely to be controversial.

With its aura of secrecy and double dealing, the confidential report is one of the least defensible methods of performance appraisal. As a motivational tool its effect is nil, since in the absence of specific guidelines from his boss regarding possible improvement areas, the executive who has been appraised is left to whistle in the dark. A relic of a more autocratic era, it has no place in any organization which values trust and cooperation between the members of its management team.

5. Self-appraisal. The basic philosophy of all self-appraisal systems is that communication and teamwork are more likely to improve if the subordinate is given an opportunity to assess his own performance. It is an admirable concept. It makes a clean break with the extremely forbidding 'prisoner at the bar' atmosphere which haunts so many conventional systems and provides both the means and the opportunity for a really frank discussion.

Self-appraisal works best where it forms part of an overall Management-by-Objectives approach to performance appraisal. Unless specific objectives have been established against which the subordinate can measure himself, the subsequent discussion with his boss is unlikely to be fruitful. It is, of course, equally unlikely that both men will interpret the subordinate's results in precisely the same way, but at least their discussions will tend to be more rational and objective than in a situation where no clear-cut standards exist. However, no system has yet been devised which cannot be defeated by bad management, and self-appraisal is no exception. For example, if the manager handles the meeting in an autocratic manner or if the company climate is still basically authoritarian, then self-appraisal will be seen by employees as simply another gimmick. Nor does it afford any protection against the wildly immature subordinate who views every facet of his performance through rose-tinted spectacles—though clearly it provides his boss with a splendid opportunity to bring him down to earth.

In 3M we have been using an 'appraisal preparation form' (see Fig. 4.1) based upon self-appraisal principles, since the beginning of 1971. It is com-

24

pleted by the subordinate a few days in advance of his appraisal interview and in most cases provides a useful input to the discussion on his performance. It has certainly helped to improve the atmosphere in which these interviews are held and has moved them nearer to that ideal two-way interchange of views which occurs all too rarely in many orthodox systems.

6. Management by Objectives. This is still potentially the most effective method of measuring performance, even it it has not lived up to some of the more euphoric claims of its early practitioners. In theory at least, the idea that a man's performance should be judged by his results is virtually unarguable: it is entirely in tune with the meritocratic temper of our age.

Nevertheless the MbO approach poses some pretty searching problems to its adherents. First, there is the question of whether the objectives set for a man are the right objectives. Do they really reflect the true priorities in his job? Are they sufficiently challenging? Does he have the necessary authority to act? Are his resources adequate? If circumstances over which he has no control change, are his objectives adjusted accordingly? If such considerations are glossed over or swept aside, the MbO-style appraisal quickly degenerates into a do-it-yourself hangman's kit—no wonder that so many experienced managers view it with suspicion! It is the old, old management story of fine tools being ruined by bad workmanship. The failure of MbO systems to take root in many companies is often more of a reflection upon management practice than upon the inherent weaknesses of the system itself.

Make no mistake: MbO does *not* remove the need for a manager to make judgements about his subordinates' performance—it simply provides him with a rational method of making them. Indeed, far from giving him an infallible slide rule, it ruthlessly exposes the quality of his thinking. Under MbO more than under any other appraisal system, the truth of the old management saw that 'every appraisal is an appraisal of the appraiser' becomes self-evident. For if the ability to set clear-cut, demanding objectives is a potent indicator of a manager's calibre, his judgement of achievement is no less revealing.

In 3M Management by Objectives is practised throughout the company but it is not a uniform centralized system which requires constant monitoring by the personnel department: it depends for its effectiveness upon the managers themselves. The principles are the same in all divisions but the application of those principles is left to the divisional manager's discretion. In this way, hopefully, we retain that flexibility of action without which MbO can so easily become just another heavy-handed control system.

In conclusion, the important thing to remember about all appraisal systems is that we are still operating in the area of fallible human judgement, *not* scientific measurement. The idea, propounded by some over-zealous pundits, that a man's performance can be measured like a roll of cloth would be laughable were it not so dangerous. It behoves every manager to approach

25

Fig. 4.1

Name	Employee No.	Location
Manager	Interview scheduled at .... D/M/Y	

APPRAISAL PREPARATION FORM

In the space above you will see that an appraisal discussion has been arranged for you at the date and time indicated. This meeting will give you an opportunity to discuss your job and your objectives during the past period.

The purpose of this form is to give you some guidelines for the discussion in order that you may derive the maximum benefit from it. It asks you to comment on those results with which you are most pleased and those which you consider less satisfactory, and to think of the reasons for this performance. You are also asked to give some consideration to your future and the kind of work you see yourself doing in five years' time. Your comments are also invited on more general aspects of your work in the company.

You may use the form or not as you wish. If you do use it, it will certainly help for a full and detailed two-way discussion about your work. At the end of the meeting you may keep the form, hand it to your manager for filing in his records or discard it.

We stress that the meeting is being held for your benefit; we consider it of great importance both for yourself and for the company. In the course of the discussion you will be told what your performance rating is for the current period and you will have the opportunity of commenting in writing on the appraisal form, if you wish.

1. With which of your results are you most pleased and why?
2. With which of your results are you least pleased and why?
3. How do you think you have improved in general performance during this period?
4. What main difficulties did you have during the period in achieving results?
5. If there are any other accomplishments you achieved during the period over and above your key responsibilities which you think may be of interest, record them here.
6. Which aspects of your job do you find most satisfying?
7. What kind of work would you like to be doing five years from now?
8. What suggestions do you have for making 3M a more satisfying company in which to work?
9. What action do you feel you or your management should take during the coming period to make yourself more effective?

26

such problems in a spirit of intellectual humility rather than with overweaning confidence. Too many so-called 'high flyers' crumble under the challenge of adverse circumstances (and too many 'no hopers' blossom under more enlightened supervision) to let us keep any illusions about the finality of human judgements. This is one aspect of management in which we are all still serving our apprenticeships.

5

How to select a
training professional

When I entered industry seventeen years ago, training was a very neglected and impoverished function which led a somewhat obscure and precarious existence at the outer fringes of either works management or personnel. The modern training professional was virtually unknown. Frequently, those in charge of training were in the evening of their working lives: many, for example, were ex-foremen whose main concern was the training of apprentices. Management training was still in its infancy and, even in the more progressive organizations, the training of supervisors was largely confined to the basic TWI programmes and the occasional work study appreciation course.

While it would be untrue to suggest that such conditions no longer exist anywhere in the UK, there has been, during the past seven years, a marked improvement in the status and scope of the training officer's job. The old-style general training has dissolved into various specialisms, each with its own methodologies and techniques; many young graduates now view a period in training as a valuable part of their career development; and whole new training empires, complete with programmed instruction and CCTV, have risen, phoenix-like, from the embers of the old TWI courses. Today, no large organization considers itself mature unless it employs at least one senior manager at corporate level to plan and coordinate the activities of this vigorous young giant. Training has indeed travelled a long way from those days when it was placed, in all but a tiny handful of companies, very distinctly below the salt.

Demand tends to generate supply, but at present the number of really experienced, all-round professionals in the training field is still relatively small. The result is that many firms are confused and uncertain when making training appointments, since there are no long-established yardsticks upon which they can draw for guidance. This leads some, in despair, to revert to the former practice of appointing 'the devil we know'—an existing employee, perhaps with little or no experience of training, who appears to be sufficiently articulate and acceptable to do the job. Other companies advertise for behavioural scientists who, it is hoped, know what makes people tick. Both of these methods have enjoyed only limited success. Since the status of any function is largely dependent upon the calibre of the people who are in it, it is important that the selection of training personnel is carried out as objectively and systematically as possible.

The purpose of this chapter is to offer as a basis for discussion five criteria for use in the selection of training officers, whether from within a company or from outside. They are based upon two major assumptions:

▶ that in the 'seventies and 'eighties training will continue to be, as it was in the 'sixties, an important growth area within industry—needing to attract men of high potential if it is to maintain its current impact upon line management;

▶ that training will offer an increasingly sophisticated range of opportunities to those who see it as a *career*.

The five criteria are: education, experience, knowledge, abilities and personal qualities.

Education

The requirement here can be stated quite simply: the training officer should be a *graduate*. There are two main reasons for this: the changing nature of his job and the increasing movement of graduates into senior positions in line management. While there are many capable training officers who are not graduates, they are invariably men who would have gone to university if they had been in a position to take advantage of the much wider opportunities which are available today.

The modern training officer, especially in the management field, needs to be an intellectual as well as a doer—able to think analytically and creatively and to understand and interpret complex ideas and philosophies. And since these are precisely the qualities which are necessary to obtain a good degree, it follows that such men are most likely to be graduates.

The subject of the degree is in no way critical—I have often found psychologists to be more at home in dealing with abnormal rather than with normal behaviour! However, given a straight choice between two candidates of equal calibre, with arts and science degrees respectively, I would choose the humanist—if only because he would be likely to be more tolerant of human cussedness (an essential attribute of any successful trainer).

There is also an increasingly important political factor: by 1980, the majority of men in senior and middle management posts will themselves be graduates. Unpalatable or not, the old saw about birds of a feather is as true for industrial management as for other professions. Graduate line managers will feel more comfortable when talking to graduate training officers and, because of this, will tend to place greater weight upon their advice and recommendations. Again, this is a totally predictable consequence of the advances in higher education which have taken place during the past two decades.

Experience

Anyone who presumes to teach in industry must himself have experience which is of value to others—otherwise he will be regarded as a blatant theorist, a man of straw, lacking both knowledge and understanding of real-life problems. It follows that training is no place for inexperienced fledglings; generally a man needs at least four or five years' industrial experience before he can deal confidently with managers and supervisors on training courses. If he has managed to obtain a junior management post during this period, so much the better; if not, he should certainly be able to provide evidence of a steadily rising level of work.

Assuming, then, that a candidate knows little about training, what other kinds of experience would be useful? To answer this question, we must look at one of the essential requirements of the training officer's job. Regardless of the type of training or the level of his 'pupils', he will always be required to influence and persuade people *over whom he has no direct line authority*. Any previous job which has involved him in doing this can therefore be counted as relevant experience. Service in such areas as sales, marketing, work study and project engineering is particularly useful.

As for the experienced candidate, the problem is to assess both the relevance and depth of his past experience in relation to the current requirements of the job—not overlooking the fact that a good performer will always seek to expand the boundaries of his job and to increase his range of responsibilities. The selector should therefore seek concrete evidence of the man's achievements, paying particular regard to areas of innovation and creativity, as opposed to those items which merely involved the maintenance of a well established system. The two major experience requirements—organizing and running courses and the analysis of training needs—should therefore be critically examined in the light of these criteria.

Knowledge

For a junior post which may be open to candidates with no previous experience of training, it is obviously unrealistic to expect a sophisticated knowledge of current thinking and techniques. Nevertheless, if a man claims to be enthusiastic about the job, it is reasonable to suppose that he will have made an effort to acquire some background knowledge and general information. For example, what previous inquiries has he made about a career in training, either by talking to trainers within his own company or by contacting an appropriate external organization such as the IPM? Has he read any relevant books or articles on training—if so, what were they, which did he find most interesting and why? What really motivates him to want the job? Where does he see it leading him? Why does he think that *he* would be suitable? An experienced candidate naturally merits a somewhat rougher ride, since one can reasonably expect him to have made every effort to keep abreast of new developments in his field. For example, a would-be management training officer who has never heard of T-Groups or Herzberg or who has never run a group discussion on a case study is unlikely to prove good material. Sometimes, a little tactful probing in these areas can produce curious results. One candidate whom I recently interviewed for a fairly senior post claimed to have enrolled for a course of lectures to be given by the late Douglas Mac-Gregor!

Such lightweights are easily eliminated from further consideration: it is the apparent professional with a sound record of previous experience who merits more serious investigation. Again, taking management training as an example, one would expect a strong candidate not only to be knowledgeable about current trends in the behavioural sciences but also to have formed rational opinions on their implications for organizational climate and management style. In other words, the selector should be constantly seeking evidence of independent thought and judgement—not merely the ability to parrot the latest buzz words from the *Harvard Business Review*.

Abilities

A training officer at any level succeeds or fails by his ability to communicate, primarily in speech but often in writing too. Even with an inexperienced candidate, it is safe to assume that, if he cannot succeed in selling himself at an interview, he is unlikely to be transformed when he is in front of a group. Listen to him carefully as he answers your questions. Is he completely audible? Does he have a pleasant and varied tone of voice? Does he speak at an acceptable speed? Would he, in short, be boring or interesting to listen to? Be alert, too, for any physical gestures or mannerisms which may indicate the degree of his enthusiasm and sincerity—after all, one would expect such a man to be animated rather than wooden in his behaviour.

All of these factors, of course, apply with even greater force to the experienced candidate, for he has had many more opportunities of practising his communications skills and it is fair to judge him by a higher standard. However, an effective trainer needs to be not only a skilled presenter of information: he must also be able to deal, authoritatively and persuasively, with tough, aggressive questioning of his ideas and with strong, and sometimes abrasive, personalities in the training group.

Fig. 5.1 Management Training Manager: Man profile

Requirement	Essential	Desirable
Education	Graduate	1st or 2nd Class Honours Degree
Experience	Minimum of seven years' industrial experience, of which at least three years must have been spent in the personnel and training field. Experience in running in-company management and supervisory training courses. Experience in analysing training needs and in designing training programmes.	Experience in a large, marketing-oriented organization, operating in competitive industrial markets. Experience in line management, especially in sales or marketing. Experience in selection interviewing for management and supervisory jobs. Experience in designing and implementing M b O programmes.
Knowledge	Knowledge of principal management and supervisory training techniques, e.g., lectures, discussion group leading, case studies, business games. Knowledge of current thinking and trends in management education, e.g., behavioural science application, performance appraisal.	Knowledge of modern decision-making techniques, e.g., Kepner-Tregoe. Knowledge of marketing and sales management including sales training techniques. Knowledge of computer application in marketing, sales and personnel fields. Knowledge of elementary statistical techniques.

Abilities	Ability to present ideas and information clearly, logically and enthusiastically.	Ability to write clear, concise and persuasive memos, letters and reports.
	Ability to influence and persuade senior management to accept new methods and techniques.	Skill in interviewing, especially for selection and counselling purposes.
Personal	Clear, logical mind with marked analytical abilities.	Innovative and creative approach to training problems.
	Forceful and enthusiastic in pushing his ideas.	Tactful and diplomatic.
	A self-starter—able to initiate and carry through projects with minimum supervision.	
	Able to establish effective working relationships with all levels of management and supervision.	
	Patient and resilient, able to persist in the pursuit of long-term goals.	

If the selector wishes to test the man's abilities in this vital area of the job, he should temporarily assume the role of a devil's advocate and deliberately challenge some of the candidate's most strongly-held views. If the man loses his temper or his self-confidence, it would clearly be most unwise to appoint him: the same applies to the shallow individual who instantly back-pedals on his principles at the first sign of opposition. What one is looking for essentially is the ability to remain composed under pressure and to continue a discussion in a logical and persuasive manner. Where there are sufficient candidates to justify a WOSB*-style selection procedure, this can often be an extremely useful method of assessing a man's leadership skills in group discussion.

Personal qualities

The assessment of personality characteristics is a notoriously difficult task and it is all too easy to specify criteria which would be more appropriate to a saint or a superman than to an ordinary, fallible human being. Moreover, the training officer's role is a peculiarly exacting one, calling as it does for a subtle combination of instructional, counselling and personal selling skills. Suffice it to say that a trainer is unlikely to be successful unless he is:

1. **Enthusiastic.** If a man is not forceful and sincere in presenting his ideas, then he is unlikely to convince anyone else that he ought to be taken seriously.

2. **Clear thinking and analytical.** Fools rush in, but skilled trainers do their homework. A training programme which is not based upon a penetrating analysis of needs and priorities is, at best, window dressing and may even be damaging to the organization.

3. **Patient and persistent.** People rarely change quickly. While spectacular breakthroughs do sometimes occur, training is mainly a war of attrition against established ideas and practices, requiring infinite patience.

I know of no infallible method of detecting these qualities in a selection situation, although the group selection and devil's advocate techniques, referred to earlier in this chapter are often helpful in revealing sincerity, enthusiasm and leadership qualities. As with any type of selection process, the more skilled and experienced the interviewer, the more likely the candidate is to relax and to express himself freely. Skill in interviewing is, however, useless unless it is backed up by detailed knowledge of the job: this requires both a job description and a man profile. An example of a man profile for a senior management training post in a large organization is shown in Fig. 5.1.

* War Office Selection Board.

34

Conclusion

During the 'seventies, it is likely that there will be substantial changes in the training officer's role—changes which will result in his operating more as an internal consultant and change agent, less as an instructor. This trend is already apparent in some organizations, especially those which have made a sustained effort to secure the acceptance of training as an integral part of the responsibilities of every manager and supervisor. From the training officer's point of view, this is an exciting development which holds much promise, both in terms of greater job satisfaction and the ability to influence events at the policy, as well as at the operational, level.

The speed of this advance will largely depend upon how quickly top management is prepared to recognize the full potential of the training officer's contribution. This, in turn, will depend upon their assessment of the calibre of the people who are in training posts. It follows that the selection of training staff is a task which requires the same care as is normally taken when appointing men to key jobs in line management. As in any area of selection, tomorrow's successes and disappointments will reflect the decisions which are taken today.

6

How to avoid losing talented people

One of the characteristics of the effective executive is his emotional self-discipline, his ability to remain calm and rational in situations where lesser men lose control. Significantly, one of the leading modern texts on decision-making is called *The rational manager*:* the whole emphasis of the book is upon logical analysis and the careful checking of facts and assumptions. All this is to be commended, for if management is still far from being an exact science, it cannot afford to be less than systematic. And yet there is one topic which, above all, provides a searching test of a company's devotion to the fashionable deities of logic and reason: company loyalty and the whole question of a man's psychological commitment to his present employers.

Good company men and true

Not surprisingly, this is a subject which many senior executives find difficult to discuss objectively. After all, a manager's decision to invest his talents in a particular company is rarely made on rational grounds alone; nor does it merely represent a simple response to the basic need to work in order to survive. It illustrates above all his *judgement*, his assessment of the kind of environment in which his skills can flourish and in which his expectations, both material and psychological, can be fulfilled. And the longer a man stays with a company, the greater is the probability that he will seek to protect his investment (in his own judgement) by reacting sharply to any criticism of his company, whether from within the organization or from outside. For many long-serving managers, their companies can do no wrong. Such sentiments may or may not be magnificent: they can hardly be called rational.

Nevertheless, if it were only a matter of simple jingoism, born of mutual affection, such attitudes would be harmless. The danger is that all too often

* Kepner, C. H. and Tregoe, B. B., McGraw-Hill, 1965.

36

they lead to an unjustified complacency, resistance to change and a blind refusal to face reality. To such managers, those who criticize the company from within, however constructively, are simply 'rebels', 'misfits' and 'moaners' who are wilfully trying to 'rock the boat'—a kind of fifth column. And when these attitudes are strongly entrenched at the highest echelons, as sometimes happens, they can quickly denude a company of its brightest young talent. Time and again an able young executive leaves a company because he feels like a still, small voice crying in the wilderness of an organization which has no idea how to use him correctly and efficiently. And all too often, when his decision to leave becomes known, the dreary mechanism of the self-fulfilling prophecy begins to operate. 'Aha', cry the 'loyalists', 'we knew this would happen. The man is clearly unreliable and has no loyalty. What we need here are good company men.' The fact that many of these so-called 'company men' would have the greatest difficulty in obtaining better jobs elsewhere is conveniently overlooked. And yet this is surely the heart of the matter. A man who would be hard pressed to improve his prospects on the open market is not entitled to feel morally superior to a colleague who moves for precisely that reason. Both men are merely following their own best interests.

Nevertheless, some organizations have an apparently unquenchable gift for creating the very conditions that lead to a continual exodus of their most talented professionals. Oblivious of the current scramble for executive talent, they continue to act as though such men were industrial Trappists, able to exist solely on a diet of job satisfaction and occasional pats on the back. They overlook, for example, the fact that a high-calibre man regards his salary as a yardstick of the extent to which his achievements have been recognized; and that he is extremely vulnerable to the enticements of the Executive Appointments columns and to the succulent blandishments of the 'head hunter'. And if the company's reward system takes no account of this—if it is insensitive to the implications of market scarcity and to the necessity to pay a premium to retain the cream of the company's talent—then such an organization must not be surprised if it ends up by preserving the purity of its salary structure, while at the same time suffering a continual 'brain-drain' of its most talented employees.

A company is only as good as the people within it: it will only grow if the people within it grow and if it can attract and retain a sufficient number of staff with truly outstanding growth potential. It is high time that those executives, who affect to be shocked whenever a high-calibre man leaves their companies, came to terms with the harsh realities of the management job market and faced up to the fact not merely that you get what you pay for, but that in some cases you may have to pay a little more—sometimes a lot more—in anticipation of what you hope to get and to retain what you have. Such firms should spend less time in complaining about disloyalty and devote greater effort to injecting an element of realism into their salary structure.

Sermons about executive morality are no substitute for a competitive reward system.

'It's up to you'

This is not simply a problem of tomorrow: it is with us *now*. At a recent management conference, I heard a speaker say that the bright young men who are now leaving the universities and business schools are demanding much more specific information about their career prospects before they will agree to join a company—that they are much less willing than their predecessors of twenty years ago to be fobbed off with such vague wafflings as 'it is up to you', 'all promotions are on merit', and all the other palliatives and bromides which so often signal the lack of a coherent career development policy. I am sure that the speaker was right and that companies which are seriously interested in attracting high-calibre people—in other words, those wishing to survive—are going to have to be much more explicit in committing themselves when confronted by those awkward questions about pay and prospects. Surely any high-potential employee already knows that it will be 'up to him' to perform if he is to win a prize? But what are the prizes and when is the prize-giving likely to be—to the nearest year, perhaps, if not to the exact day? And what is the point of telling such a man that 'all promotions are on merit'? It simply provokes the unspoken response: 'I should damn well hope so.' How fatuous can you get? The fact that such meaningless statements are still made points to the endemic weakness of some organizations in their total human resources planning: the continuing refusal to take management manpower forecasting and succession planning really seriously. 'Sufficient unto the day is the evil thereof' is about as far as they have got—especially those who are still labouring under the burden of what has been so aptly termed 'the arrogance of past success', instead of focusing on tomorrow.

Increasingly, many professional managers have a common reference point which is independent of their present employers: their current value in the executive labour market. Whether or not we approve of this development is irrelevant; we have to come to terms with it, instead of indulging in futile Canute-like postures which inhibit realistic thinking and decisive action. We must recognize, too, that many professional management skills are highly transferable and that sometimes a man's interest in this particular specialization transcends his attachment to an individual employer. Nevertheless, every man has a right to expect a company to make some attempt to fulfil his reasonable needs and aspirations in the light of his demonstrated performance and potential. And if that recognition is not forthcoming and the man leaves, then it is quite useless to complain about 'disloyalty' as if he were a feudal chattel, a serf bound by mysterious spiritual chains engraved with a particular company's name.

Loyalty—on both sides—is something which has to be *earned*, not something which can be taken for granted as an eternal right implicit in every employment contract. I am not, of course, referring to the commoner and narrower obligation which rests upon every employee to preserve the confidentiality of his company's policies, plans and processes—or, indeed, of any information which could benefit a competitor. My concern is with the much broader question of a man's personal psychological commitment to a company and with the development of more rational attitudes and concepts. After all, times have changed. Talent is at a premium. Executive mobility has become a major factor in industrial life—the dramatic growth of selection consultancy during the past ten years provides ample evidence of that. You keep those whom you *deserve* to keep.

Motivational exchange

For me, one of the most encouraging developments in British industry in recent years is that more and more progressive companies are developing a noticeably more businesslike attitude to loyalty based upon the realization that essentially it involves an *exchange of assets* between the man and the company. These organizations offer demanding and challenging jobs, a very informal and friendly company climate and a remuneration and benefit package which is as competitive as they can make it. In return, they expect a man to throw himself into his job with enthusiasm and dedication and to use his knowledge and skills to the fullest extent of his abilities. This seems to me a more rational approach than to talk about loyalty as though the company were some kind of Aztec deity and the employees were human sacrifices.

Part 2

What every line manager should know

7

How to develop managers on the job

Compared with the continual and unpredictable challenges which a manager faces in his job, many management development courses are only a pebble on the beach of his experience. True, he may be stimulated or rejuvenated by the intellectual adrenalin of a course which is relevant to his needs, yet he is rarely transformed in any permanent way, nor is it realistic to expect such miracles. For like any other organism, he works—and develops—within a total environment which consists partly of the opportunities and satisfactions provided by his job and partly of the constraints imposed by his own intelligence, ability, motivations and drive.

Most experienced managers recognize this intuitively; hence their scepticism towards the pedlars of managerial wonder-drugs, especially those whose expertise has been forged in 'the groves of academe' rather than in the more rugged battlegrounds of profit responsibility and tigerish competition. Douglas McGregor's celebrated observation that 'managers are grown, not manufactured' is one that few managers would dispute, since it accords with the visible realities of executive life. Nevertheless, a manager's development on the job cannot simply be left to chance: it must be systematic not casual, controlled not chaotic, planned rather than merely haphazard. If managerial success must inevitably depend upon the survival of the fittest, then the task of management development is to ensure that there are men fit enough to compete.

How can managers be effectively developed on the job? How can their experience be broadened so that they become generalists—businessmen—in outlook, rather than specialists whose attitudes are determined by the needs of their function instead of by the needs of the firm? What techniques are available to achieve these objectives, and what benefits can be expected from them? These are the questions which this chapter will seek to answer.

43

Planned delegation of responsibility

Just as every manager regularly reviews the performance of the machines, materials and equipment for which he is responsible, so too, he should periodically assess the strengths and weaknesses of each of his immediate subordinates. Next, he should examine each of his own responsibilities and ask himself the following searching questions:

Why do *I* do this?
Who among my subordinates could do this for me *now*?
Who could do it after suitable coaching and training?

Together with the assessment of his subordinates' strengths and needs, the answer to these questions will indicate the kind of job experience which each individual needs to become a more effective employee. The manager should then set himself a number of specific delegation goals to promote the development of each of his immediate subordinates. These will, in turn, be reflected in the subordinates' personal goals and progress can be monitored at regular intervals.

The effectiveness of planned delegation largely depends upon the attitudes of the manager who is delegating and the abilities and motivations of the subordinate. Some managers fear to delegate because of the risk of mistakes, particularly in the short-term; others betray their personal insecurity by attempting to veil their jobs in a shroud of secrecy which, they imagine, makes them 'indispensable'. In fact, these tactics are much more likely to make them unpromotable. A manager cannot reasonably expect promotion if he has not developed someone capable of taking his place. Unfortunately, industry is littered with such men who loudly complain of their lack of advancement, apparently untouched by the thought that the remedy is in their own hands.

The benefits of a systematic application of planned delegation throughout the management structure are summarized below.

To the manager who is delegating: better performance, more highly-motivated subordinates and greater all-round management strength. Above all, more time in which to plan and to innovate.
To the subordinate: an opportunity to 'grow' and to obtain greater job satisfaction.
To the company: the assurance of a continuous supply of managers who are developing their abilities in meeting new challenges under realistic operating conditions.

Special projects

This method is a refinement of planned delegation, though frequently broader in scope. It is a particularly effective technique for developing ambitious, high-

44

potential employees with a capacity for original thought and highly-developed analytical abilities. It is also an excellent method of testing for the presence of these qualities.

The aim of the project method is to provide the individual with a specific and important problem to investigate, the solution of which will make a measurable contribution to the efficiency of his unit. Such problems are often recurring ones which the boss himself has not had time to investigate in depth; normally, they require the subordinate to obtain and analyse a variety of information (preferably from outside as well as from within his own department) and to present written recommendations for improvements. The project is carried out in addition to the subordinate's normal duties against an agreed target date—which should not be too generous.

The advantages of the method are:

1. It challenges an individual's desire for achievement and recognition by providing him with an important practical problem to investigate and solve. (On no account should it be 'made work'.)
2. It broadens his thinking and experience beyond his own specialist boundaries.
3. It tests and develops his reasoning abilities and involves him in the discipline of setting down his conclusions and recommendations in writing.

Every manager with high-potential subordinates should consider the use of projects as an aid to development on the job. They can, of course, be carried out by groups as well as by individuals.

Coaching

Personal coaching of subordinates by superiors is most frequently used to focus an individual's efforts upon the need to improve in a specific area of his performance. The superior, having noticed a deficiency, continues to point it out as it occurs and—primarily by asking questions—helps the man to work out his own solution for overcoming it. Coaching can be a most rewarding technique because it keeps the development activity realistically associated with the job. It does, however, require considerable skill and self-control on the part of the superior, who must avoid 'preaching at' his subordinate and allow him reasonable time to work out his own improvement plans—especially when changes in attitudes are involved.

Departmental meetings

This technique is often associated with the project method; the individual who has completed a project presents his findings at a departmental meeting and then leads the subsequent discussion period. It can, however, be used to inject fresh enthusiasm into the efforts of almost any subordinate, particularly those who have grown a little stale through over-exposure to the same kind of work.

Each subordinate either selects or is assigned a specific subject (normally, but not necessarily, related to his present departmental responsibilities) and is given a deadline to meet for presentation of his findings at a departmental meeting. The method forces the individual to reflect upon and classify his experience, to search for new information and to suggest viable improvements to present policies, methods or procedures. The fact that his presentation takes place before his peers, as well as his superior, introduces a competitive element to which even a moderate performer usually responds. Like special projects, such assignments are carried out in addition to the individual's normal duties.

Follow-up after courses

When a subordinate returns from a training course, the superior asks him to submit a report outlining what benefits he believes he obtained from the course and his plans for applying what he has learned to improve his performance in his job. The boss, of course, should have previously satisfied himself that the course was relevant to his subordinate's needs and should be in general sympathy with the concepts taught. Following the presentation of the report, both men meet to establish an action plan for the implementation of those ideas which they agree to be feasible. The superior then monitors progress in the normal way. Provided that the course has been well-chosen and that the subordinate recognizes its relevance to his needs, this technique can be very effective in improving performance. It relates theory to practice in terms of an agreed plan of action and, above all, demonstrates to the subordinate his superior's interest and involvement in his development.

Job rotation

This method involves an individual in a series of planned job changes in order to broaden his experience. He takes over a job which he has not previously performed and stays in it either for a definite period or until his superior is satisfied with his performance.

Job rotation is a powerful method of preparing high-potential specialists for future general management responsibilities. It does, however, require meticulous planning, and it is vital to ensure that the rotated manager exercises real responsibility and is not merely a glorified observer. The reactions of managers who are not selected for rotation must also be anticipated. Job rotation is essentially a calculated risk, an investment in future performance. A company embarking upon it must be prepared to tolerate short-term losses and in-efficiencies while the newcomer adjusts himself to the requirements of his job.

Membership of committees

This technique has some of the broadening effects of job rotation, though usually on a more limited scale. The selected individual joins a special-purpose committee, either within or outside his own department, to broaden his experience or to acquire experience of another function, e.g., a production man may join a marketing committee, or vice versa.

The method is particularly effective when the individual is assigned a specific area of responsibility on the committee and is not merely an observer, and when the committee is composed of representatives from a number of functional groups across the whole company. In my own company, during the past year, we have established a sales management council which consists of the senior management of our various product groups. At least twice a year, the council meets for a joint three-day conference with the top executives who comprise the company's management committee. The frank exchange of views which takes place on a whole range of topics pertinent to the achievement of the company's sales and profit targets have undoubtedly improved communications and teamwork and have imbued everyone concerned with a greater sense of purpose.

Conclusion

In this chapter, I have outlined some of the practical techniques which are available to companies wishing to 'grow' their managers effectively in their jobs. Underlying each of these methods is the conviction that the primary requirements for effective development are a challenging job which stretches the manager's abilities and enables him to acquire new knowledge and skills, and a demanding but understanding superior who sets high standards and is conscious of his responsibilities for developing people.

There are no panaceas in management development, no magic elixirs which can transform ugly ducklings into swans. But just as both ducklings and swans operate in a common element—water—so all managers are bound by a responsibility to meet the requirements of their jobs. It is in the job environment, ever the most practical of business schools, that the main development effort must be made. After all, the job like the poor, is always with us.

8

How to follow up after courses

Sending a manager on a course is a business investment. Whether the objective is for him to acquire new knowledge or skills or to modify his present attitudes, the pay-off to the company lies in the extent to which his performance improves.

In the case of courses which aim to teach or to improve specific elementary management skills, the problem of measuring results is not too difficult. For example, if a manager is weak in his ability to speak effectively in public or to chair meetings or to write clear, concise letters and reports, the effect of the training should be apparent within a few weeks of his return from the course; any improvements in his performance are quickly noted by his superior and also by his colleagues and subordinates. The continuing popularity of courses in communication skills stems not only from industry's conviction of their importance: it is also appreciably easier to measure whether in fact the company has received 'value for money'.

This is certainly not the case with general management courses, particularly those in which the main emphasis is upon such behavioural skills as human relations, leadership and 'motivation'. Here we are in the realm of intangibles, of conflicting attitudes and approaches, where the entrenched concepts of a managerial lifetime are exposed to the searching fires of analysis and appraisal. The same is true of courses dealing with management principles and practices. Once again, the primary aim is to unfreeze a manager's thinking by a series of planned injections of new ideas and information which, it is hoped, will modify his customary responses to a variety of managerial problems and situations.

Attitudes, however, are notoriously difficult to change, especially in the case of the older manager. And when they are deeply embedded, as they so often are, they represent a sizeable investment of a manager's ego—of his basic perceptions of what management is about. It would therefore be unrealistic to expect such sudden and spectacular improvements as are commonly noted following training in communications skills. The time span of change is inevitably much longer and improvements are correspondingly more difficult to assess.

Two areas of improvement

Nevertheless, depending upon the innate capacity of the individual manager and the strength of his personal drive to attain high standards of performance, we would eventually expect to see evidence of improvement in two main areas: *thinking ability* and *management ability*.

Evidence of improved ability to think clearly, rationally and systematically can be detected in a number of ways. For example, there is the manager who begins to display a noticeably more challenging approach to his job, becoming more analytical and constructively critical of existing methods and routines. He is less ready to take 'no' for an answer, begins to ask more questions about the purpose and objectives of his assignments and is manifestly more creative in his decisions. He also shows a greater readiness to offer his boss solutions to problems, or recommendations for approval, instead of simply presenting him with problems for solution. And in doing so he marshalls his facts more effectively, shows greater evidence of having considered in depth the various alternative courses of action and defends his judgements objectively and without excessive emotion. Very often he will have set down his analysis in writing as an aid to mature evaluation and judgement—a far cry from the days when he would simply have rushed into his superior's office with a 'bright idea'.

Clearly, such a manager is going through a process of rediscovering the challenge and excitement of his earlier days in management; and while there are many factors in any situation which can help to produce such behaviour, one certainly cannot exclude the stimulus of a course which he found truly relevant to his needs.

Evidence of improved management ability can be demonstrated by a manager's greater concern with the 'why' rather than the 'how' of his job. Superiors may find themselves requested to give clearer statements of objectives, of performance standards and of the authority which they intend should be exercised in the execution of particular tasks. Sometimes a manager may present his superior with a new or revised job description as a basis for discussion and clarification of these matters: this in turn provides a first-class opportunity for setting key objectives and developing action plans to achieve them. Many managers also begin to show a more planned approach to the use of their time and an altogether keener appreciation of those areas of performance which will produce the best results for the least cost.

Along with increasing evidence of a more systematic approach to their work, such managers also exhibit a greater desire to be trusted to get on with the job and to report to their superiors only when things go wrong. Reporting by exception is, of course, very much in the superior's interests as it allows him precious time to carry out his own responsibilities for planning and innovation. It should therefore be encouraged at a pace consistent with the subordinate's ability to recognize situations which unmistakably require his boss's intervention.

More willing cooperation with superiors and colleagues and more conscious efforts to get to know them are further typical examples of the impact which an effective course can have—particularly upon a manager who has hitherto shown little awareness of the importance of human relations skills. These modifications in attitudes can also have repercussions upwards: such a manager will undoubtedly expect a greater readiness on the part of his superior to consult him about changes that will affect him and to permit him to participate in those decisions where he has knowledge and experience to contribute. This is further evidence to the superior of his subordinate's developing maturity as a manager and of his desire to make a fuller contribution to the performance of the unit in which he operates.

The boss's role

The most important single factor in determining a manager's post-course performance is, in fact, the behaviour and attitudes of his immediate superior. If the boss has attended the same course and is enthusiastic about its teachings, the probability is that the pace of improvement will be accelerated considerably. If he has not attended the course but is eager to evaluate its impact, he must be prepared to play a more patient, subtle role. Some superiors prefer to discuss the course on the basis of a formal report which the manager produces soon after his return. Others prefer an informal chat during which they probe for changes in attitudes and specific plans for improvements. There are others who, unhappily, display no interest whatever, give the impression that they consider the course a waste of time and make it plain that they expect 'business as usual' with no rocking of the boat by 'untried theories' or 'risky innovations'. Only the most highly motivated managers can withstand this kind of reception and in such cases the chief effect of the course is to build in frustration, which in turn results in lower morale and apathetic performance.

Assuming that the course has been carefully selected for its relevance to the manager's needs and that his superior agrees with its teaching, the most suitable role for the boss is that of the interested, sympathetic coach who is keen to encourage his subordinate to apply whatever he has learned in a realistic, practical way. The manager's ideas and suggestions should be examined critically but sympathetically and, where they appear to offer tangible benefits, plans for improvements should be agreed and implemented. Only by such a mutually supportive and participative approach can the full bene-

50

fits of the course be reaped to the advantage of both the company and the individual.

The attitude of mind which should underlie effective coaching is one which some managers do not find easy to achieve, since it requires them to relinquish their formal hierarchical role and to learn to perceive situations and problems *as they appear to their subordinates*. Without this kind of empathy and self-control, the manager's attempts at coaching may appear to a subordinate as mere inquisitions or 'pep-talks' in which all the communication is strictly one-way. In his approach to the challenge of coaching, the manager should frankly recognize those things which are susceptible to change and those which are not. Frontal assaults upon a man's personality characteristics or personal values are the surest way of inducing defensive mental postures, even though these may be disguised by the mask of formal acceptance. By the time a man enters industry, he has already been exposed to most of the great character-forming experiences of his life and his personal values will be constantly reinforced by the human predilection for selecting such evidence as he perceives to support them. Coaching, like politics, is the art of the possible. In Drucker's phrase, it is a question of 'building upon strengths'.

Above all, coaching is not brainwashing or mere manipulation. True, it has a business rationale: the improvement of performance and results. But it springs primarily from an attitude of mind which recognizes that ultimately a man can only be helped to help himself—and from the conviction that there is no nobler managerial task than that of helping another human being to develop to the limits of his potential. The effective coach is therefore 'long' on questions and deliberately 'short' on answers. He seeks not to impose his own 'canned' solutions to problems, but to ask those questions which will lead the subordinate to deduce for himself the action required. The power relationship between boss and subordinate is an inescapable fact of organizational life; if handled crudely, it can quickly become a destructive rather than a constructive force. The most effective coaching, therefore, is that which poses questions rather than imposes solutions, suggests rather than concludes, subtly teaches rather than mechanically preaches. It provides a searching test of a manager's maturity and of his intrinsic respect for the worth of another human being.

A heightened awareness of changes in attitude, a willingness to encourage a manager's efforts to improve and early recognition of his achievements—these are the prime requisites for a superior who wants to obtain a sound return from the investment of time and money which a course represents. Post-course enthusiasm is a tender plant which quickly dies if exposed to the twin frosts of cynicism and indifference. But given the right stimulus and support from his superior, there should be no reason for the returning manager to be tempted to echo Longfellow's plaintive cry: 'I shot an arrow in the air. It fell to earth, I know not where.'

9

How to delegate effectively

As an organization expands, as jobs grow bigger and more demanding, so managers at all levels begin to find it increasingly difficult to cope with the growth of their responsibilities. In this time of technical and scientific revolution, with new techniques mushrooming every day and everywhere, it is no longer possible to run either a company or a department as a one-man band. So the manager finds that he has to delegate more and more of his work to the people who report to him. In other words, he authorizes them to do work for him that he would otherwise have to do himself. Sometimes, this is not enough and it is necessary for additional staff to be recruited to deal with the complexity of a particular job which, perhaps only a short time ago, was of seemingly little significance. In both cases it is clear that, without effective delegation, there can be no real progress. For both companies and managers, effective delegation provides the life-giving oxygen needed for survival and growth.

Unfortunately, in the eyes of some managers and their subordinates, delegation is synonymous with 'passing the buck'. Nothing could be further from reality. When a manager assigns a responsibility to a subordinate, he cannot thereafter wash his hands of it and take no further interest, because he remains accountable to *his* boss for the performance of his *total operation*—not simply for the work which he continues to carry out himself. This is a vitally important principle of management that every manager should—indeed *must*—recognize, accept and apply; without it there would be organizational anarchy, since it would be impossible to exercise effective control and coordination at any level in the enterprise. Nevertheless, for many managers, delegation is what the psychologists call an 'emotive' word—that is to say, one which triggers off an irrational reaction, based on unfortunate past experience which they can remember only too vividly. Some, for example, have bitter memories of having been hurled into the perilous waters of a new assignment without any sort of training or preliminary briefing; they were simply left to sink or swim. Others can recall the frustrations which they experienced when confronted with the kind of roadblocks that spring up all too quickly when insufficient authority has been delegated, or when the relevant policies and procedures have not been made clear. It follows, then, that delegation, if it is to be effective, must be properly planned and properly thought out. Otherwise, the result will be loss, waste and a good deal of human bitterness and ill-feeling. This, in turn, may seriously undermine the normal working relationships between a manager and his team.

So what are the components of effective delegation? How can a manager win the respect and confidence of his subordinates so that they apply themselves enthusiastically to the tasks which he has delegated, instead of approaching them with apathy or suspicion? Here are four key principles of delegation which, if consistently applied, will produce the required results.

Set clear objectives

No man can be expected to display enthusiasm for a job which seems to have no purpose or rationale; he will look on such a task as a totally meaningless chore or, worse still, as an insult to his intelligence. If the manager who is delegating does not take the trouble to clarify the end-results which the assignment is planned to achieve, then he will deservedly fail to motivate his subordinates to perform effectively. For he will be treating them no better than if they were inanimate objects without wit, sense or feelings, and he cannot therefore complain if he is rewarded with performances which are devoid of initiative or, indeed, of any kind of personal commitment.

An effective manager spells out the objectives as a matter of course. He uses clear, specific language, not vague generalizations, and is careful to express the required results wherever possible in precise, quantitative terms— for example, x increase in sales, y decrease in costs, z improvement in delivery times, etc. Moreover, he talks enthusiastically to his subordinate about the benefits to the company, the department and, not least, to the man himself— for some men do not always appreciate that successful completion of an important new assignment will give them valuable additional experience or improve their prospects of advancement. The manager *never* concludes his discussion of the objectives without agreeing with his subordinate upon a sensible target date for the completion of the task, so that the man can make the necessary adjustments to his current work priorities. To summarize, the manager plays in turn the roles of teacher, salesman and colleague, because he has learned that this is the way to motivate the vast majority of normal human beings, whereas highhanded autocracy would result merely in sullen acquiescence and apathetic performance.

Grant adequate authority

If a manager fails to delegate sufficient authority to a subordinate to enable him to carry out an assignment, then he has no right to be indignant if the results are disappointing. And yet most of these problems of inadequate authority stem, not from conservatism or malice on the part of the boss, but from his failure to think clearly about the various situations that his subordinate will encounter. For even the most apparently straightforward instructions often require a surprising amount of authority to enable them to be executed. Consider, for example, this typical conversation between a supervisor and an operator in a busy engineering workshop:

Supervisor (agitated): 'See this part I'm holding, Joe? I want you to make another six like this by four o'clock this afternoon. Sooner if you can—they're screaming for it in Assembly. Sorry to have to ask you, but Ted Banks in A section is off sick and we've no replacement.'
Joe (glumly): 'OK. I've never made one before, but I'll do my best.'
Supervisor (relieved): 'Good. Over to you then.'

Just look at the different authorities which Joe might need in order to meet his deadline. He might, for example, need authority to:

1. Obtain a drawing from the drawing-office files.
2. Draw material from the stores.
3. Draw special tools.
4. Use a special lathe.
5. Use additional electric power.
6. Visit parts of the factory which are normally out-of-bounds to him.

If he does not already have all the necessary authorizations (and there is no reason why he should since he has never done the job before), then he will certainly be hindered and delayed when he attempts to carry out his task—indeed, until he has obtained the authority, he may not even be able to start. And yet, ironically, if he does manage somehow to produce on time the supervisor will have been protected from the consequences of his own incompetence and will no doubt continue to consider himself an excellent leader of men. No wonder delegation is an emotive subject—on the shop floor and in the office, as well as in the ranks of management! Let us be absolutely clear on this point: it is the responsibility of the man who is delegating to anticipate just how much authority his subordinate will need, and to give it to him—not to fling him willy-nilly into a kind of minefield where every step he takes is subject to frustration and delay.

Clarify policies and procedures

When delegating, a manager should always ensure that his subordinate knows and understands those company and departmental policies and procedures, written or unwritten, that provide the practical framework within which he must act. The prime effect of any policy or procedure is to limit the choice of actions which can be taken in a particular situation—to specify the boundaries which must not be crossed.

Just as in cases of inadequate authority, any lack of clarity in communicating policy is almost certain to sabotage effective delegation and to lead to inefficiency, waste and considerable ill-feeling. If the relevant policies are badly communicated, then subordinates will unwittingly exceed, or fail to use, their authority. This, in turn, will result in constant mistakes and frequent reprimands which will be much resented by men who feel not unreasonably 'more sinned against than sinning'. And the more often this happens to a subordinate, the more quickly he will become cynical and disillusioned and begin to lose both his enthusiasm and his initiative. Indeed, very soon he will have *no* initiative and such phrases as 'I'm not going to stick *my* neck out' will spring all too readily to his lips.

It cannot be repeated too frequently that policies and procedures can only serve their legitimate purposes when they are properly communicated to the people whose responsibilities are affected by them. Failure to do so will not only undermine the effectiveness of the policies: it will create suspicion of management's intentions.

Provide effective training

It goes without saying that no act of delegation can hope to succeed unless the subordinate involved has the necessary competence to make sensible use of the authority which has been granted to him. 'I'd like to delegate more of my work but I have no one sufficiently capable to delegate to'—this is the great rallying-cry of so many managers for whom delegation is a kind of managerial beatitude. A laudable, praiseworthy ideal, but one that has little connection with the harsh realities of business life.

Clearly, if a subordinate lacks the ability to make a success of an assignment, that is a perfectly valid reason for his boss to decide against delegating. But this is not the end of the matter—it is merely the beginning. For there are a number of searching questions which any manager faced with such a situation must now begin to ask himself, such questions as:

1. Why is it that my subordinates lack the necessary ability?
2. Am I selecting the right people? If not, why not?
3. Am I giving them adequate opportunities to acquire the knowledge and skill which they require?

4. Do I take an interest in their progress and try to pass on my own know-ledge and experience?

5. Do I encourage them to develop themselves—perhaps, by taking appro-priate courses of study in their own time?

If you have a subordinate with a clearly identifiable weakness—a specific deficiency of knowledge or skill—then it is your responsibility *as a manager* to initiate the action necessary to bring about an improvement. This is a cardinal principle of effective management. Depending on the nature of the weakness, you may either choose to deal with it yourself by coaching him personally on the job, or it may be necessary to seek specialist help from with-in or outside the company. The vital point is that nothing is likely to happen unless you, the boss, try to *make it happen*. A manager is even more account-able for making optimum use of his staff than he is for obtaining the required standards of performance from materials and machines, since ill-trained and poorly-motivated people are unlikely to make proper use of the resources under their control. Effective training and development of his subordinates lies right at the heart of every manager's job. It is not an optional extra or the sole prerogative of training specialists.

Conclusion

Delegation is not simply a parrot-cry of the management theorist: it is the lifeblood of any truly dynamic enterprise which is committed to growth. A manager who refuses to delegate is not only hampering his company's pro-gress—he is also conniving at his own stagnation, since he can hardly expect advancement unless he has trained a competent successor to take his place. Effective delegation, properly planned and systematic, offers opportunities to people throughout an organization to acquire new skills under realistic operating conditions. It is a tool of development which no professional manager can afford to ignore.

10

How to avoid becoming out of date

Despite the proliferation both of courses and institutions, it will always be necessary for managers to accept a measure of responsibility for developing themselves. Indeed, the degree of enterprise and initiative displayed in a manager's own self-development efforts is an excellent indicator of his potential for advancement. And since management responsibility invariably requires a manager to adopt broader and more flexible attitudes than in his earlier career as a functional specialist, he needs exposure to a wider range of ideas and experience. This means, in turn, that he must be prepared to learn from the experience of others, be they academics, consultants, research workers or—most valuable of all—experienced fellow managers. One of the most relevant and effective ways in which he can tap these various sources of expertise is to undertake a planned management reading programme.

The operative word is, of course, *planned*. There is a bewildering variety of books to choose from and, unless he approaches his task systematically, there is every possibility that the manager will quickly become confused and disillusioned. As with any other type of management problem, he will not make much headway unless he has clarified his objectives and, in particular, has decided just how much time he is willing to invest in his reading programme.

The manager who is a newcomer to the world of management literature will be wise not to set his sights too high and to allocate his time initially to a few recognized 'classics' in his chosen field, instead of squandering his efforts on a much larger number of books, many of which, inevitably, will be second-rate. A busy manager who is already fully stretched by the operational requirements of his job should not attempt to read more than one or two really first-class books each month, unless there are urgent reasons (such as an imminent promotion to a completely new field) for a more accelerated pace. Too ambitious a schedule, even if the diet consists only of the most carefully-chosen books, will soon result in mental fatigue—for management literature, unlike most fiction, requires a capacity for sustained analytical thinking and a clear and alert mind.

Having defined his objectives and determined the amount of time that he is prepared to allocate to his reading schedule, the manager's next step is to select the books that he intends to read. There is no need whatever for him to wander disconsolately around the bookshelves of the local library; there are plenty of sources to which he can turn for help. For example, if the company has a training officer, he will often be able to provide much valuable advice and guidance on the most suitable books and where they may be obtained; if not, the information departments of the larger professional institutions are usually very willing to help.

The library of the British Institute of Management has for many years operated a loan service of books and articles which is available both to individual members and to the personnel of companies which are collective subscribers to the BIM. In addition, the BIM Publications Department has produced a large number of checklists and information summaries on management techniques which are normally supplied free of charge to members. There is also much to be said for the manager who actively seeks advice from those of his colleagues who are knowledgeable and experienced in the field in which he is interested. Few managers can resist the compliment—and challenge—to their expertise which such a request implies.

How can a manager make the best use of his reading time? And what steps can he take to ensure that the information which he wishes to acquire is absorbed and retained? There are a number of different strategies that can be followed and, while all require self-discipline and application, the selection of a particular strategy is largely dependent on the individual manager's own temperament and personality.

Some managers like to see tangible evidence of their reading efforts, and consequently produce their own written summaries of each book's key chapters and main ideas. Others read slowly and carefully, pausing frequently to ponder how a particular idea or approach might be applied to their own jobs. Yet another device, favoured by many managers, is to discuss the ideas gained from their reading with colleagues or subordinates, either by introducing them casually into informal conversations, perhaps over a drink or at lunch, or by raising them formally at departmental meetings as a basis for action on a current problem.

The most important factor, however, is not the strategy itself but the sustained effort which underlies it. For unless the manager is constantly striving to relate what he is reading to his past experience or to his present problems, it is unlikely that he will derive much benefit from the time which he has invested. This, in turn, is a major reason why he should not attempt to absorb new ideas and information when he is mentally fatigued or when he is likely to be frequently interrupted. An hour or two of quiet reading at home, or in the reading room of the local library, will be worth more than a month of effort on crowded commuter trains and buses.

During the course of a year, I deal with a large number of requests for reading programmes from managers in my own company—often men who have been recently promoted to senior management posts in which man-management and organizational skills are far more important than expert technical knowledge of a particular function. Invariably, these men are already under considerable pressure in adjusting to their new responsibilities and, while not wishing to dampen their enthusiasm, I normally prescribe a fairly limited initial schedule of about half-a-dozen books, mainly general-management 'classics' that have had a marked influence on modern managerial thought and practice. A typical six-month programme for a newly appointed manager would consist of such books as:

1. *The practice of management* by Peter F. Drucker, Heinemann, 1955.
2. *The rational manager* by Charles Kepner and Benjamin Tregoe, McGraw-Hill, 1965.
3. *Improving business results* by John W. Humble, McGraw-Hill, 1968.
4. *The human side of enterprise* by Douglas McGregor, McGraw-Hill, 1960.
5. *Exploration in management* by Wilfred Brown, Heinemann, 1960.
6. *The computer in society* by Brian Murphy, Anthony Blond, 1967.

Occasionally, I receive requests from managers for further clarification or discussion of some of the ideas which they encounter during their reading. Increasingly, however, these systematic reading programmes are being incorporated in managers' individual career-development plans and the follow-up becomes part of the immediate superior's responsibility for ensuring that the total plan is carried out. For example, managers are sometimes asked by their superiors to give short presentations on their reading at departmental meetings; each talk is then followed by questions and discussion. More frequently, however, the books form part of the preparatory work involved in a special project that has been assigned to a manager for the purpose of developing his abilities in a specific area of his job. This is by far the most effective course of action, because the manager's incentive to learn from his reading is heightened considerably if he recognizes its relevance to his current responsibilities and objectives.

Planned reading programmes, carefully tailored to an individual manager's needs, can make a worthwhile contribution to a manager's self-development efforts. They cannot, of course, transform his performance overnight for, as with any development technique, much depends upon the attitudes of the manager being developed, especially his willingness to apply himself systematically to the task of broadening his knowledge and of reassessing his existing beliefs and prejudices. Nevertheless, given positive attitudes on the part of the manager and his boss, they can be a valuable source of new ideas and can also help to recharge a manager's mental batteries by encouraging him to reflect upon his experience. During the next decade, management jobs at all levels are likely to become increasingly complex and demanding, and managers will be constantly challenged by the need to keep abreast of new concepts and techniques. A good book may or may not be, in Milton's phrase, 'the precious life blood of a master spirit'. It is nonetheless unquestionably a most useful aid to any manager who is concerned with improving his performance and thereby developing his potential for advancement.

11

How to be a more effective manager

Every manager must keep abreast of the relevant management techniques in his field; to neglect to do so is to invite managerial obsolescence and loss of respect. Good management, however, is not simply a matter of techniques, important though they are to the solution of specific problems. It is a question of having the right attitudes to the job, to one's boss, to one's colleagues and to the people one controls. These attitudes must be converted into actions that in time develop into a recognizable management style so that the manager is— and is seen to be—rational, consistent and methodical rather than emotional, unpredictable and haphazard. This chapter discusses five principles of good management that are essential to effective performance.

Every manager and supervisor, regardless of function, has a common obligation to use his resources as effectively as possible. If he is to do this, he will need to be adequately equipped with, and to use, three main tools—knowledge, intelligence and personality. The effective manager, therefore, is constantly seeking—and creating—opportunities to develop himself so as to ensure that:

1. His knowledge is sufficient to enable him to test the validity of information and advice;
2. His intelligence is trained to make the best use of his knowledge, so that his decisions are sound;
3. His personality is such that he can persuade his subordinates to carry out his decisions willingly.

To achieve this requires great self-discipline, even greater patience and an ability to remain resilient and philosophical in the face of those disappointments and setbacks that are an inevitable part of managerial life. Nevertheless, progress towards greater effectiveness need not, and should not, be solely a matter of blind chance or of continual trial and error. There are a number of basic principles of good management which, if recognized and consistently applied, will enable a manager to arrive at his destination by high-speed motorway rather than by meandering country lanes.

Define your objectives

A manager who consistently manages in the light of clearly defined objectives is far more likely to produce worthwhile results than one who merely reacts to events at random. Not only will he make more economical use of his resources, but he will also experience the incomparable psychological satisfaction of controlling his own destiny. It is now generally recognized that many of the most common 'executive-stress' diseases—for example, coronary thrombosis and nervous breakdowns—are caused not so much by hard work as by feelings of helplessness and inadequacy in the face of a seemingly unpredictable and uncontrollable work environment. Management by Objectives does not remove these pressures, but it does make them tolerable and allows them to be seen in perspective, without fear and without constant feelings of insecurity.

Understandably, the advocates of MbO systems have laid much emphasis on such measurable improvements as increased profits, lower costs and greater all-round productivity. This is to confuse cause and effect. The outstanding benefit of MbO, from which all others are derived, is that it increases a manager's *self-confidence* in facing the uncertainties of the future and enables him to predict, plan and control his activities to a degree that he may previously have thought impossible. When a manager—indeed, when any human being—begins to recognize that he can influence his environment, he is motivated to operate at the upper rather than at the lower limits of his potential. No more can reasonably be asked of him, nor should he be satisfied with less.

Improve your communications

A manager spends most of his time in communicating with other people—with his boss, his subordinates, his colleagues in other departments, and often with suppliers, customers and government officials. Unless he is competent in the skills of personal communication—whether it be running or contributing to meetings or writing letters and reports—he will not succeed in marketing either himself or his ideas. No matter how keen his native intelligence, he will not be recognized as an effective contributor. Fortunately, such skills can be acquired by intensive training and constant practice.

What cannot be acquired so easily is a basic attitude towards communicating that goes far beyond the possession of personal skills—one that penetrates the inner citadel of a manager's fundamental beliefs about the nature of his job. Increasingly, in modern industry, information is not merely the raw material of decision-making, it is an instrument of power. Those who possess it can, by the use they make of it, win or lose customers, persuade or alienate colleagues and make or break the careers of others. Some managers, often motivated by feelings of personal insecurity, deny to their subordinates information they need in order to do their jobs. Others habitually 'filter out' all unwelcome information before communicating with their superiors, hoping that the omissions will remain undetected until far into the future and perhaps, with luck, for ever. A manager who persistently indulges in such practices is unfit to hold his job, for he is acting as dishonestly as if he were tampering with the petty cash or falsifying his company's accounts. Cash can be replaced but morale, once undermined, is far more expensive to restore.

The mature manager regards information as a resource to be distributed rather than as a weapon to be wielded in his own self-interest. 'Who needs to know this?' is the question uppermost in his mind when he receives information that is not strictly confidential to him or to his own level of management. Being a Machiavellian communicator may occasionally pay off in the short term, but it is unquestionably a certain recipe for long-term disaster, and for the simplest of reasons. A manager who denies information *to* others will be denied it *by* others. Gradually but inevitably this will affect the quality of his decision-making and his results. He will become ever more isolated within the organization until, perhaps, in despair, he resigns or is dismissed.

Be jealous of your leadership

If a manager cannot lead—if he cannot persuade other people to do willingly what he would like them to do—then he is failing to meet the most important requirement of his job. Being an effective leader does not mean that a manager must be either a superman or a saint; it does mean that he must be trusted and respected. This, in turn, requires him to be consistent and predictable in his methods of managing so that his subordinates can use their initiative and make decisions without constantly wondering how the boss will react. An insecure subordinate will always tend to 'play it safe', and when such a virus spreads throughout an organization, scything initiative and creativity wherever it penetrates, then the days of that organization as a competitive force are numbered.

A good manager, therefore, is always jealous of his leadership. If, for example, he learns that his subordinates are persistently seeking advice and guidance from someone other than himself, whether from within or outside his department, then he regards it as a personal defeat and as evidence of a serious failure in his leadership of the group. Sometimes, of course, it may be that intense and sustained pressures of work have made him less accessible to his subordinates and have created the impression that he is indifferent to their problems. Alternatively, he may have been genuinely concerned to avoid appearing to 'breathe down their necks'. Whatever the cause, he will recognize that the situation will not change unless he himself is prepared to invest more time in his personal relationships with his subordinates, so that he establishes himself as the captain of a team rather than as a remote deity handing down instructions from Olympus.

Write down your plans

Most managers attempt to plan their work because without plans it is impossible to establish effective controls. All too often, however, these plans remain in their heads and are not committed to paper. This is an extremely hazardous practice that leads to many operational problems which could have been foreseen and dealt with if the plan had been written down and reviewed, coolly and analytically, by the manager concerned. The human brain is just not programmed to carry a mass of complex detail; it becomes overheated, confused and is too easily distracted from primary objectives. Many managers subject themselves to quite unnecessary pressures through their preference for indulging in complicated mental gymnastics, instead of applying the simple but effective discipline of writing down their objectives and plans.

The objection may be raised, of course, that there is just not enough time to do these things, and that, anyway, the average manager has to deal with far too much paperwork already. But as Drucker pointed out some years ago in *The practice of management*, 'There is never a shortage of time; there is only a lack of priorities'. Unless a manager gets into the habit of programming his work and of writing down his plans (in whatever note form he may find convenient), then the really important matters will be neglected and he will spend his life dealing with urgent trivialities. The manager who spends the bulk of his time 'fire-fighting' is unlikely to think clearly, to plan effectively or to operate as an efficient leader of his group.

Similarly, if a manager finds himself submerged by the paperwork arriving on his desk, he should examine each document and ask himself, 'Does this give me information that I need in order to plan or to control?' If the answer is 'Neither,' then he should take action to get rid of the document or to stop it from being sent to him. Many reports and memoranda are circulated 'for information' and do not concern many of the managers who receive them. Moreover, some managers actively contribute to their paperwork problems by calling for detailed reports and statistics that they do not really need and rarely, if ever, use. If a manager is sufficiently ruthless in eliminating such irrelevancies, he will create ample time for writing down his key objectives and detailed plans and, above all, for thinking creatively about the future.

Build for the future

A wise manager recognizes that his future progress is linked with the performance of his subordinates and that boss and subordinate alike have a common interest in continued self-development. An executive should be judged not only by his current work results but also by the durability of the organization which he builds while in office, and by the calibre of the people he develops to take his place. Too many managers are judged in terms of short-range gains and improvements that may have been achieved largely at the expense of the future stability and efficiency of their departments.

John E. Bugas, a former Vice-President of Ford Motor Company, once proclaimed that 'no man is fit for promotion until he has trained his successor', and it is true that many managers fail to be promoted because of lack of competent replacements. It is extremely shortsighted for any manager to neglect the development of his subordinates because, quite apart from the possible effect on his own promotion prospects, he will soon find that the performance of his group will begin to deteriorate as people quickly sense his lack of interest in their progress.

All businesses have a common interest in survival and the manager who delegates sensibly and who systematically prepares his subordinates for broader responsibilities is making a powerful contribution to this most basic of company objectives. There can be no greater tribute to a manager's effectiveness than a department that continues to run smoothly after he has moved on.

Conclusion

In 1733 a writer named John Ford produced a treatise for London businessmen which he described as 'a serious address to men in business, concerning the right ordering of their affairs; with advice in the case of those who have unhappily mismanaged'. The following extract contains as much good sense and wisdom as any modern textbook on management:

> Undertake no more than you can manage.
> Perform with delight and a kind of unweariness.
> Be watchful over strangers.
> Trust not your memory, but immediately make entrys of things in the
>   proper books.
> At proper times inspect your affairs.
> He who observes the rules laid down will be likely to thrive and prosper
>   in the World.

From 1733 to 1975 is indeed a long haul but the fundamental principles of good management have not changed to any radical degree since men first faced the problems of organizing and motivating other people to accomplish objectives. Specific management techniques may blossom and fade but the basic job of managing is as old and as complex as the nature of man himself.

12

How to improve your leadership ability

The success of any manager in his job depends to a considerable extent upon his ability to gain the cooperation and goodwill of the people whose work he directs. This, without question, is the most exacting of all managerial tasks, but it is essential that the effort be made simply because today there is no real alternative, quite apart from ethical considerations.

Leadership by threat or by the whip—if you can call that leadership—is no longer expected or accepted. People within companies will not stand for it; they either leave or become increasingly disgruntled and resentful. And the effect upon the company's external relations is equally costly; any personnel officer can testify to the repercussions upon recruitment, particularly among high-calibre men who might otherwise have been attracted to the company.

Developing the right attitudes

It follows that the modern manager needs to be a much more perceptive leader than his predecessor of thirty or forty years ago. He has to deal with an infinitely more complex situation which requires a whole range of subtle psychological insights and motivational skills. He has to know his men as individuals, know what they are looking for, know what makes them tick. They constitute his most precious resource, and his own results—and therefore his own accountability—will be vitally affected by the enthusiasm (or the lack of it) with which they throw themselves into the tasks which he has delegated to them. Without an understanding of the temperaments, personalities and motivations of those whom he leads, his leadership will be ineffectual —he will be operating in the dark. Moreover, it is difficult for any man to have much trust or confidence in the kind of leader who does not try to get to know him, who shows no interest in him and who appears to regard him simply as a creature of his will, a mere pawn upon an industrial chessboard.

Yet it is precisely this feeling of mutual trust and confidence which is right

66

at the heart of effective leadership in industry today. What men are looking for from their managers is, to quote Douglas McGregor, 'a fair break'—the feeling that they are being led by competent men who know their jobs and who care about them as individuals. They do not expect—nor want—to be led by men with temperaments of saints.

Much will be forgiven if they believe that their managers are men of integrity whom they can trust to make sensible decisions and to handle them fairly. *Integrity*, then, is the vital personal quality which makes one man trust another to behave honourably and compassionately; without it there is little hope of mutual respect and willing cooperation. This, in turn, can make all the difference between enthusiasm and apathy in a man's performance, between continued company expansion and loss of customer goodwill, between healthy growth and insidious decay.

So far, we have been concerned with a manager's downward relationships with his subordinates but, of course, he has other sorts of relationships: upwards with his superior, and sideways with his managerial colleagues in other departments. If we examine first the relationship with his boss, the central point for any manager to grasp is that the sole reason for the existence of his own job is to help the boss to achieve his objectives. After all, if the boss were able to do everything himself, if he had not been forced to delegate certain responsibilities owing to the volume or variety of the work, or for other reasons, then there would be no subordinate job. It is therefore the subordinate's duty to be *helpful* to his boss. One way in which he can be extremely helpful is to learn to communicate effectively with him, whether orally or in writing. For just as the subordinate will appreciate clear definitions of his responsibilities and authority from his boss, so in turn he must give his superior all the information which he requires in order to be able to plan, control and coordinate effectively.

A typical communication problem—one which, if handled badly, is fraught with frustration for both parties—is the situation where the subordinate has a proposal for an improvement which he is anxious to persuade his boss to accept. Time and again such ideas, whatever their intrinsic merits, fall on barren ground because of inadequate preparation and ineffective presentation by the enthusiastic, if impetuous, subordinate. It is simply not realistic for the latter to expect that the boss will instantly grasp his idea and see its brilliance right away; he needs it presented to him in a businesslike manner with clear-cut details of costs and of the benefits to be gained, as well as some indication of the shortcomings of the existing method.

It is a denial of elementary business logic—indeed, of common sense—to expect a manager to be motivated to take action on a proposal which, for him, deals with a nonexistent problem. All too often he will suspect that he is being asked to sanction 'change for the sake of change'. Fortunately, however, these vital skills of personal communication—effective presentation of ideas, letter and report writing, contributing to meetings, etc.—can be taught

67

fairly easily and the resultant benefits, both to the individual and to the company, are often truly remarkable.

In just the same way, a manager must be able to communicate effectively with other departments of the organization, especially those whose work is interlocked with his own. In practical terms, this means that he must be prepared—and organized—to pass on, promptly and accurately, all the information that they need from him. Poor or slipshod communications are often responsible for much of the ill-feeling that exists between related departments in many large and medium-sized companies. Each side suspects the other of trying to sabotage its results, sometimes by passing on information which is inaccurate or incomplete, but more frequently by failing to communicate at all until an emergency situation has developed.

At the root of this internecine feuding is a failure to recognize what being helpful really means. It is more, much more, than a question of having a pleasant attitude to others, or of feeling committed to company objectives, important though these factors are. It is a question of realizing that just as no man is an island, so, in modern industry, no *job* is an island and that, where jobs are interconnected, the need for promptness, accuracy and reliability in passing on relevant information is paramount.

The question may be asked: 'What has all this to do with a manager's leadership responsibilities?' The answer is clear and straightforward. When a manager is recognized as being a good communicator, people—whether it be his boss, his subordinates or his colleagues in other departments—respect him. And when this happens it means—unmistakably—that they are acknowledging his *capacity for leadership*.

Developing the right skills

During the past forty years, there have been many attempts to define the personal qualities and characteristics needed for effective industrial leadership. Most of these studies resulted in long lists of qualities, which, in effect, demand that managers should be either saints or supermen—and preferably both. This search for an ideal personality specification—the so called 'trait approach'—has long since been abandoned for, as R. F. Tredgold commented in his book *Human relations in industry*: 'The longer and more comprehensive the list of qualities, the more obvious it must be that their possessor would be of no use in industry, for he would inevitably be in demand elsewhere, maybe as a prime minister—or even as an archangel.'

The modern approach to leadership is essentially pragmatic: its basic tenet is that the kind of leadership which is appropriate to a particular situation depends very much on the nature of the situation itself. Only one personal quality is regarded as mandatory—integrity; without this, there can be no question of mutual confidence between the manager and those whom he leads.

But what practical steps can a manager take to create a climate of mutual trust and respect? How can he generate confidence in his integrity? Here are six basic principles which if practised, sincerely and consistently, will produce the desired result.

1. **Show that you know your job.** Technical competence in one's field invariably commands respect, even if, *by itself*, it is not sufficient for effective leadership. After all, a star salesman does not necessarily make a good sales manager. But there can be little confidence in a manager who cannot give sensible guidance to his subordinates when they approach him to discuss problems or to seek advice. Many managers are today feeling the pangs of technical obsolescence, due largely to their failure in the past to keep abreast of new ideas and techniques. The manager who wishes to progress—indeed, to survive—must be prepared to accept a measure of responsibility for his own development by reading widely in his field and by constantly seeking to improve established practices and methods.

2. **Be frank.** Keep your subordinates well informed, particularly about important changes in policies, routines, methods and procedures that will affect their work. And tell them as early as possible—not at the last minute. Above all, always try to show them how they will benefit, e.g., how the proposed change will make the job easier to do or make it more interesting or give them the opportunity to gain valuable new experience. Talk 'benefit language'.

Similarly, let each man know how you view his performance, both strengths and weaknesses, and what you consider he should do in order to improve. Most important of all, tell him what steps *you* propose to take in order to help him. Be constructive.

3. **Be a good coach.** Working under a good boss is by far the most effective training that any man can have—the kind of boss who passes on his knowledge and experience, who sets realistic standards of performance and who takes constructive action to ensure that his subordinates attain these standards. Such a man is no mere order-giver; his relationship with his subordinates is essentially that of a coach who recognizes that the development of his human resources is a vital part of his managerial responsibility.

4. **Be firm.** Stand up for what you believe to be right. This does not mean be obstinate or pig-headed. Having listened carefully to anyone who possesses knowledge or experience which is relevant to the problem, a good manager goes ahead and makes *his* decision. He does not, for example, allow himself to be discouraged or diverted by people who pour cold water over his ideas, simply because they are afraid of change. Nor, having made his decision, does he spend time worrying about all the other alternative courses of action which he might have taken.

An effective manager must learn to tolerate uncertainty—the uncertainty of waiting until it is clear whether his decision was the right one or not. Remember, the higher a man progresses in management, the longer these periods of uncertainty become.

5. Be impartial. Never play favourites or allow your personal reaction to a man to influence your objectivity in assessing his performance. Nothing will destroy a manager's prestige more quickly than the suspicion that he has hidden standards—that he assesses men on the basis of whether their faces 'fit' rather than in terms of their results.

6. Know people—and be known. You cannot lead if you are, in effect, a faceless man sitting behind a desk; you need to get out of your office and get to know your subordinates as individuals. Similarly, go out of your way to meet all the other people you need to know—the key figures in other departments whose work is interlocked with yours. And be prepared to take the initiative in making yourself known; call on *them*, instead of simply leaving the first contact until the moment arrives when you want something from them. If you create your own opportunities in this way, the people concerned will remember you and are likely to be a good deal more cooperative in the future because you broke the ice.

Finally, there is one other requirement for effective leadership which may at first sight, appear curious: a good manager must be a *sensitive* man. This does not mean that he must be a *prima donna* with a temperament like a yo-yo; it means that he must be sensitive to his *environment*—to what is going on around him, to the temperaments and feelings of the people whom he is required to lead and to influence. Such a man will, for example, be capable of detecting subtle changes in attitudes, perhaps in the absence of any concrete facts.

Furthermore, and not least, he must be sensitive to the kind of impact which he himself makes upon other people. For if it is fair to postulate that a leader must be a mature person—and, surely, it is—then he must quickly acquire a capacity for *self-awareness*. Because the total impact of his own personality—his attitudes, manners, tone of voice and many other aspects of his personal behaviour—will be of considerable importance in determining whether or not he obtains the cooperation that he needs in order to perform effectively in his job.

Effective leadership in industry is primarily a matter of the sustained application of ordinary common sense, coupled with an appreciation of the motivational mainsprings of human behaviour. It does *not* require a manager to be a psychological expert or to have the virtue of a candidate for canonization. If a man is willing to reflect upon and to learn from his experience, if he is willing to see the other man's point of view, then he will become progressively more competent with the passing of time. Integrity, sincerity, flexibility—these are the essentials for lasting success.

Further reading

Adair, J., *Training for leadership*, Macdonald, 1968.

Blake, R. and Mouton, J., *The managerial grid*, Gulf Publishing, 1972.

Brown, J. A. C., *The social psychology of industry*, Pelican, 1970.

Drucker, P. F., *The effective executive*, Heinemann, 1967.

Farnsworth, T., 'Coaching: The buck stops here', *Management in Action*, August 1974.

Follett, M. P., *Dynamic administration*, Pitman, 1973.

Gellerman, S. W., *Motivation and productivity*, American Management Association, 1963.

McGregor, D., *The human side of enterprise*, McGraw-Hill, 1960.

McGregor, D., *Leadership and motivation*, MIT Press, 1966.

Tredgold, R. F., *Human relations in modern industry*, Duckworth, 1963.

13

How to write realistic job descriptions

Like any other tool of management, job descriptions can be so misused and distorted that they become drained of useful purpose and have no real impact on performance and results. Many, for example, are far too lengthy, consisting of elaborate accounts of operational methods and techniques. Others consist simply of a list of tasks, both important and trivial, and make no attempt to define the key results to which the tasks are, presumably, related. Worse still, many descriptions, once written, are rarely if ever reviewed, so that they quickly become mouldering historical documents rather than practical working tools. For all these reasons, job descriptions have had a somewhat chequered history in both UK and US organizations. It is still comparatively rare to find them regarded as a really helpful aid to effective management.

This is somewhat surprising since there are many useful purposes that job descriptions can serve, quite apart from their primary role of clarifying responsibilities. For example, they can be of great value in such important areas as:

Selection (including internal promotions). Job descriptions help to increase the objectivity of selection procedures by providing common standards against which the qualifications and experience of candidates for vacant posts can be assessed.

Performance appraisal. The assessment of a man's performance is likely to be considerably more accurate if his results can be measured against written statements of his responsibilities and specific improvement targets.

Training and development. A comparison between the on-going requirements of the job, as set out in the job description, and the results achieved during a given period can often highlight the training and development needs of the job holder. This, in turn, provides a sound basis for future development activities, both on and off the job.

Organization planning. When it becomes necessary to make changes in the organization structure of a working group, a study of the relevant job descriptions can provide a clear and comprehensive picture of how the various key responsibilities are currently allocated.

Job evaluation. Where an organization has a salary structure based on job grades, it is necessary for the content of a job to be analysed and evaluated in order that it be placed in the appropriate salary group. The job description plays a vital part in this process since it provides the data on which such decisions are made.

Nevertheless, important though they are, all these activities are relatively infrequent occurrences when compared with the kind of daily operational pressures to which managers are subjected. And this, perhaps, is the primary reason why so many companies have found that their job-description schemes have failed to take root—they have been regarded by managers as of only occasional value in certain specialized situations. The problem, therefore, lies not in producing job descriptions but in ensuring that managers *use* them—not just for certain 'one-off' purposes but continuously as a basic tool of effective management. How can this be achieved?

The first and most important point is to recognize that the vast majority of managers are pragmatic, down-to-earth people who tend to judge any management technique in terms of the practical 'pay-off' to their own operations. However discomforting it may be to the management purist, most managers simply will not read—still less, use—a job description which is lengthy, detailed or verbose. It follows, therefore, that such documents should be concise, clearly-written and, above all, *action-centred*.

This immediately raises the question of who should write the job description. Here the vital requirement is that, wherever possible, it should be produced as a result of a discussion between the job holder and his superior. If, as often happens, the description is written independently by the superior and imposed on the job holder without any prior discussion, then the latter can hardly be blamed for feeling somewhat apathetic and resentful; it is, after all, *his* job. The ideal arrangement in the case of experienced and competent men —one which secures their involvement and support right from the start—is for the superior to request the job holder to produce the initial draft of the job description. This should then be reviewed by the superior and any amendments made. Finally, copies of the agreed version of the description should be retained by both parties and a copy sent to the personnel manager for company record purposes.

What should be included in a job description? This is where many of these documents go hopelessly astray. Some are so brief as to be almost meaningless; others include so much detail that they become virtually unreadable. In the final analysis, every organization must tailor the style and format of its job descriptions to its own particular requirements. Nevertheless, there are three main areas that all descriptions must cover if they are to be useful to managers — organization structure, job responsibilities and current work targets.

Organization structure. The requirement here is for sufficient information to enable the job to be identified within the structure of the department. This means recording such details as the job title, the name of the department and the immediate reporting relationships of the job holder (see Fig. 13.1). The

Fig. 13.1   XYZ Company Limited Job Description

Section I—Job details	
Note:	The purpose of this section is to identify the job within the organizational structure of the division, plant or staff group.
Job title:	Management Training Manager.
Department:	Personnel.
Location:	XYZ House, Regent Street, London, W.1.
Reports to: (State job title)	Group Personnel Manager.
Supervises: (State job title)	Management Training Officer.
Date written:	10 December 1974.
Approved by:	W. B. Morris.
Job title:	Group Personnel Manager.

date when the description was written should also be included since it provides a pointer to the need for future review and possible amendment. All job descriptions should be checked for major changes in content at least once a year.

Job responsibilities. The purpose of this section (see Fig. 13.2) is to provide guidance to the job holder on the essential requirements of the job. These can be classified under two main headings—overall objective and key tasks.

(a) *Overall objective*. The statement of the overall objective should summarize the basic purpose of the job. It should, in effect, answer the question 'Why does this job exist?' and should clarify the job's distinctive contribution to departmental or corporate objectives.

(b) *Key tasks*. These are the major areas of responsibility and represent a breakdown of the overall objective into *sub-objectives*.

Current work targets. This is the action-centred part of the description and is intended for continuous use by the manager and his subordinates for purposes of planning, control and performance review (see Fig. 13.3). The targets are

74

Fig. 13.2   XYZ Company Limited Job Description

Section II—Job responsibilities

Note:
The purpose of this section is to provide guidance to the occupant on the essential requirements of the job.

A. Overall objective:
To coordinate and implement a company-wide management and supervisory training programme in all sales, production and staff areas up to and including senior management level.

B. Key tasks:
1. To review with senior sales, production and staff management their current departmental training needs as established by performance appraisals and other discussions on performance.
2. To develop suitable programmes of in-company training to meet these needs.
3. To ensure that appropriate education and training is provided for all employees who are appointed to a supervisory position, within one year from the date of the appointment.
4. To keep abreast of new developments in management and supervisory training techniques and to develop new in-company programmes incorporating such techniques as are relevant.
5. To design, in consultation with senior management, appropriate self-development programmes for their departmental managers and supervisors.
6. To administer and control all records of training required for both company purposes and I T B levy and grant regulations.
7. To work with the Employment Manager, and with senior divisional and staff management, to devise systematic selection procedures for appointments to supervisory positions, and to contribute advice and guidance to line management in the implementation of these procedures.
8. To maintain contact with all major institutions in the training field, e.g., B I M, the Business Schools, the Management Courses Index, etc.

---

the job holder's immediate work priorities and must, of course, be related to his key tasks. Every effort should be made to produce targets which are quantitative and therefore *measurable*. Equally important, no target is valid unless a realistic date has been set for its achievement.

As the initial targets are met, so new ones are inserted so that there is, in effect, a 'running record' of performance throughout the year. Having been involved in setting the targets, the subordinate is much more likely to feel committed to achieving them than if they had been simply imposed on him without prior consultation. This well-established link between employee

75

Fig. 13.3   XYZ Company Limited Job Description

Section III—Current work targets (1 January–1 July)

Targets	Performance review	
	Comments, Agreed action	Date

1. To have completed annual review of management and supervisory training needs by 1 February.
2. To have issued programme of in-company courses, for period 1 April–30 June, to senior management by 1 March.
3. To have prepared individual career development programmes for all managers rated as outstanding in their 1974 performance appraisals by 1 March; and to have completed similar programmes for supervisors by 1 April.
4. To have submitted recommendations for computerization of company training records to Group Personnel Manager by 1 May.
5. To have run two 'Principles of Management' courses for newly-appointed supervisors at Head Office by 1 May.
6. To have conducted two group selection procedures for potential supervisors by 1 June.
7. To have completed and dispatched the Company's 1974/5 Training Grant Claim to the I T B by 1 July.

---

participation, motivation and achievement is one that no forward-looking manager can afford to ignore.

Experience shows that the majority of managers welcome the type of practical, results-oriented job description which I have described. The benefits, in terms of improved communications and control, are so quickly forthcoming that many managers wonder in retrospect how they were ever able to manage without them. Nevertheless, as always happens when any new technique is introduced into an organization, there are always those who are reluctant to change their existing attitudes and practices. Some of the traditional objections are:

1. **'I am too busy to bother with job descriptions.'** Then *make time*—one can never be too busy to do one's job properly. A prime responsibility of every manager is to help his subordinates to achieve the results that are expected of

76

them. A man who is confused about his objectives and responsibilities is unlikely to be an effective performer; indeed, he may well spend the bulk of his time dealing with relative trivialities. And if his results are poor, then his manager will rightly be held accountable by his superior. By neglecting his subordinate's needs, he is creating difficulties for himself.

2. **'I already know what my people are doing.'** Famous last words! Scores of detailed investigations, carried out both in the UK and in the USA, have revealed that in many organizations up to 70 per cent of managers and subordinates held widely-differing views about the basic requirements of the subordinate's job. The only way for a manager to be sure that this does not apply to him is to put his beliefs to the test and carry out the kind of practical exercise described in this chapter. He could be in for some surprises.

3. **'My job changes too rapidly—a job description would be a waste of time.'** A frequent objection but one that is rarely justified in practice. Admittedly, some jobs do change more quickly than others but such changes tend mainly to affect the short-term work-targets rather than the overall objectives and key tasks. Methods and techniques, too, may change fairly rapidly in some jobs but here again appearances can be deceptive. For example, a manager may find himself using very different techniques this year, as compared with last year, in order to accomplish a key task which has remained unchanged.

4. **'I am no good at writing—and neither is my subordinate.'** Then you both have a major training need—one for which, fortunately, there is no lack of remedies. Both the British Institute of Management and the Management Courses Index will be pleased to recommend a suitable course for personnel from subscriber organizations. If this does not apply, then your company training officer or the education secretary of your professional institute may be able to help. Do not, however, exaggerate the degree of writing skill that is required. Write in a style that is simple, direct and clear. *Plain Words* (Pelican) by Sir Ernest Gowers contains a wealth of practical guidance on the principles of effective writing.

How can job descriptions be introduced into an organization? As with any major technique of effective management, it is always highly desirable for the chief executive and other members of top management to give a lead—not simply by paying lip-service to the concepts but by actually producing descriptions of their own jobs. However, there is no reason why a manager should not introduce job descriptions within his own operation, even in the absence of a company-wide programme. Indeed, it is often due to the enthusiasm and initiative of a few farsighted executives that new management techniques gain acceptance in an organization. Once the benefits of the technique become apparent, other managers are attracted to it and a 'bandwagon effect' is created which gradually permeates the whole company.

A concise job description that focuses on results can give purpose and direction to a manager's efforts. As Peter Drucker has so often pointed out, a manager may be capable, hard-working and conscientious and yet may still fail to contribute effectively to business results. A job description, in effect, provides him with a route-map that enables him to concentrate on the really significant areas of his job. There could scarcely be a more practical way of ensuring his effectiveness.

14

How to conduct effective appraisals

During the past ten years there has been a great flowering of performance appraisal schemes throughout British industry. Appearing under a variety of titles and employing an even greater variety of methods, most of these schemes aim at judging the value of a manager's work contribution, the quality or quantity of his work and his potential for advancement. Yet, even among companies which pride themselves upon their progressive personnel policies, there is an increasing feeling that performance appraisal is at the crossroads— that many systems are causing more friction than amity, more dissension than improved morale. Why?

Part of the answer lies in the kind of qualities that appraisals so often try to measure. Many companies, to judge from their assessment forms and procedures, are mainly concerned with personality and character traits such as integrity, honesty, loyalty, determination, initiative and dependability. Even job knowledge and job performance may be overshadowed in the overall rating. It is in this area of taking people apart on a personality basis that performance appraisal begins to run into resistance. Employees resent being 'psychoanalysed': managers, too, are uncomfortable when they are put in the position of 'playing God'.

Why did appraisals drift into this personality-centred approach? Partly because of the increased general interest in psychology and psychiatry; partly because of the modern emphasis upon human relations skills and the influence of leadership studies which stressed 'personality' and 'character'. But the chief reason was the practical difficulty of assessing the contributions of such men as research scientists and line or staff executives whose work performance is often more qualitative than quantitative. Lacking an objective instrument of measurement, performance appraisal fell into the quicksands of the 'trait approach'.

To recognize that personal characteristics are important is one thing: to do something about them is quite another matter. It takes a trained psychiatrist several years of sustained analysis to help a man pin down the full aspects of his personality. There is still no universally-accepted method of measuring 'character'. Moreover, such knowledge as we possess about the depths of personality formation casts considerable doubt upon the extent to which management can hope to influence or change people, using conventional appraisal techniques. After all, by the time managers enter the picture, school, family and society have had something like a twenty-year start!

Rare indeed is the manager who enjoys discussing his subordinate's personality and character 'weaknesses' in a face-to-face interview. This is not a question of moral cowardice: the respect we hold for the inherent value of the individual leaves us distressed when we must take the responsibility of judging the personal worth of a fellow man. Yet the 'trait approach' to performance appraisal forces us not only to make such judgements but also to *communicate* them to those we have judged. Does this not come dangerously near to a violation of the integrity of the personality?

Many experienced psychologists would say that it does. Indeed, some have questioned whether people really *want* to know precisely how well their boss feels they are doing and where they stand. Most subordinates, they claim, would rather be *reassured* than *appraised*: they want to hear that 'everything is all right'. This raises the further question of whether even the most constructive comments, however tactfully stated, *can* be communicated without doing more harm than good. Once again, recent studies of this problem seem to indicate that the answer may be 'no'.

The reason for this is that a man's total working effectiveness depends upon two things: his personal knowledge and skills, and his feelings about himself and his relations with other people. When his personality or character is being criticized he may suffer an undue amount of what the psychologists call 'ego loss'—in other words, he may begin to lose his self-confidence and become a less effective worker. This is a hazard which even the trained psychiatrist frequently encounters when dealing with the personality problems of his patients. How much more dangerous are the potential consequences when the task is carried out by unqualified people, however well-meaning they may be.

If we are to avoid the perils of the personality-centred approach, we need to recognize that no individual operates in a vacuum. True, he controls and is directly responsible for some aspects of his performance, but management is clearly responsible for certain other important aspects, just as the general business environment is responsible for still others. Instead of assuming that an individual is the sole master of his performance, we must acknowledge that there are many factors which are beyond his control: they are part of the organizational framework of the company which is determined by top management. Viewed in this light, the traditional one-way assessment of the individual is seen to be totally inefficient; a more realistic approach would bring manager and subordinate together for a mutual *two-way* exploration and discussion of *all* the factors which affect performance. What does this involve?

Firstly, an agreement between the manager and the subordinate on the current overall scope of the job. Much of the friction which often develops in jobs occurs because of lack of clear-cut mutual agreement on all aspects of the work that is being done or should be done. The opening phase of the discussion should therefore consist of a review of the *total work situation*. Any questions, suggestions or complaints which the individual may have should be investigated and the decisions recorded; where there is an existing job description, this will need to be expanded or revised. At this stage no attempt should be made to criticize or judge performance: the objective is to achieve a realistic evaluation of performance problems—not people alone.

The boundaries of the job having been defined or redefined, the discussion can now move on to the mutual planning of work goals. Bearing in mind that men invariably work harder to achieve targets which they have set themselves, the subordinate should be required to state the objectives which he hopes to achieve in his work programme for the next three, six or even twelve months. Here the discussion should not be confined solely to the individual's job; it should also take into account any interrelationships with other jobs in the department, division or firm. This encouragement of the subordinate to set his own work objectives does not in any way imply an abdication of managerial control: on the contrary, it makes such control easier and more effective. For in setting his own work aims—or in reaching agreement on them with his manager—the individual has, to a considerable extent, already established criteria for performance. And these are criteria which he cannot subsequently disown or reject; after all, it was he who helped to formulate them.

The final stage of this job-centred approach to performance appraisal involves a further interview between the manager and his subordinate to determine what measure of success the latter has achieved in reaching the agreed targets. Here again the objective is not merely to discuss past successes and failures but to construct a more realistic framework for future performance. Once more, the manager and subordinate, in an atmosphere of mutual confidence and respect, sit down to find answers to the following questions:

What is the situation *now*?
What can *management* do to improve it?
What can *the individual* do to improve it?

We would hope to find increased management interest in checking its own part in creating the kind of conditions that encourage top performance, with particular emphasis upon the organization of work. We would expect to find the subordinate displaying a more creative approach to his job, coupled with a greater willingness to acknowledge those aspects of his performance where improvement is necessary. We would be certain to find both manager and subordinate intensely concerned with the questions of what tasks exist and what is the best way to structure them. And, not least, we would expect increased managerial attention to be given to problems of placement and redeployment

—for in a situation where the efficiency of the organizational structure is constantly being improved, the 'square pegs' among a manager's subordinates will be easier to identify and relocate.

How does this approach affect the use of appraisals for salary review purposes? The answer is that it does not—and rightly so. To tie the granting of salary increases exclusively to the results of appraisals is not only a confusion of thought but a standing invitation to cynicism and misunderstanding. Let us consider the kind of situation which so often arises.

When a man is told that he has been rated highly on his performance appraisal, he naturally expects to be rewarded when the salary increases are handed out. Yet he may be disappointed. He may not receive the expected increase. Anyone who has dealt with the realities of salary administration, particularly in a small or medium-size firm, will know that this situation is not unusual. For, with rare exceptions, salary increases are not really made on the basis of merit alone but against a background of many factors—for example, the individual's service in the job or the length of time since his last increase. Above all, conditions may be such that there is not sufficient money available to give an increase to everyone who may deserve one; the firm's position in the market may be deteriorating with consequent strict economies on all expenditure.

It is at this point that complaints begin to be heard about the 'hypocrisy' of performance appraisal. The remedy? Surely, to be realistic, it would be just as sound to use simple ranking methods to determine *who* is *most* entitled to share in the available rewards—for that is the real nature of the decision to be made?

In this chapter I have tried to show that an individual's performance is related to a complex of factors, some within his control, others within the control of management, still others a reflection of the prevailing economic environment. Nowhere is it suggested that individual ability is not important; but the truth is that effective performance is often stifled in conditions where jobs are poorly structured or where organizational relationships are vague and ill-defined. The difficulty with many conventional appraisal schemes is that the individual is assumed to be the sole arbiter of his performance, whereas in fact it is not within his power to control all of the many factors that influence his ability to work effectively. Not least, the emphasis which such schemes placed upon personality characteristics tends to obscure the far more urgent need for a constant review of organizational structure and the design of jobs.

One final point: this results-centred approach to performance appraisal does not require managers to possess highly esoteric knowledge and skills. What it *does* require is a type of managerial sophistication which makes it possible for the manager to consider dispassionately all the factors involved in stimulating or retarding performance. Provided that he is willing to assume the kind of coaching role or relationship with his subordinates that will permit two-way communication and exchange of ideas, the method outlined here offers a broad approach to better understanding and better teamwork. For an enlightened management in an industrial democracy these are surely objectives which are worth achieving.

15

How to develop
a high flier

Strictly speaking, age has nothing to do with this aspect of performance. A man can be just as much of a high flier at 45 as he was at 25—the only difference is that he has had an extra twenty years in which to confirm his early promise. Nevertheless, for the purpose of this chapter, let us consider the high flier as a young man, of limited experience but infinite promise, whose personality and performance suggest that he is destined for the top. How can such a man be managed so that he fulfils his potential to the mutual benefit of himself and his employer?

The answer, paradoxically, is to manage him as little as possible: he just will not respond to the traditional managerial mechanisms of authority and control. Like the gifted child in the primary school class, he needs a more individual, personalized approach—one which allows him maximum opportunities for self-expression. After all, we are dealing with a man who cannot be motivated, still less manipulated: *he motivates himself*. He lives by his own standards, and these are always higher than his present performance since for him the present, by definition, must be inferior to the future. While he will welcome guidance on his objectives and priorities, he will certainly resist any attempt to impose on him an alien philosophy of work—a set of attitudes which seem to prize conformity rather than creativity and to act as a brake upon his personal development.

Even allowing for the complexity of the challenge which he represents, industry has made a notably poor show at managing the high flier. It has failed to see that *achievement* and *recognition* are the major propellants; instead, it has relied too heavily upon salary and status. These are only short-term expedients and will not permanently compensate for an unsatisfactory and frustrating job in a company which frowns upon change and discourages innovation. In such an environment an offer of more money may strike the recipient as a bribe rather than a reward and is likely to arouse feelings of contempt instead of gratitude. And if the organization's reward system is so inflexible and insensitive as to give equal rewards to the excellent and the average, it is no wonder that he quickly becomes cynical and disaffected. Many companies suffer a continuous 'brain drain' of their most talented employees because of an inability to face up to the implications of unequal performance.

It is not just that industry so often selects the wrong 'motivators': handling the high fliers also calls for a very special brand of man-management expertise, one that is exceedingly rare in modern business. The worst kind of boss for a high flier to have is the typical 'safety first' organization man who sees him as a threat rather than a challenge and who quietly buries his ideas beneath a shroud of silence or delegates them for discussion to a powerless committee. Many a high flier's resignation can be traced to the quietly effective sabotage carried out by an unsympathetic—and frightened—boss. It is precisely the *opposite* of such a man who is best at dealing with the high flier—the tough, no-nonsense executive who is prepared to tell him flatly when his ideas are impractical, and who backs up his views with well-marshalled facts and arguments. The high flier usually gets along famously with such men because he recognizes instinctively that he has much to learn from them and that they can make a priceless contribution to his maturation and development. What the high flier needs, seeks and respects is not the conventional boss—subordinate relationship but a *colleague relationship*—one which is based upon give and take, upon frank discussion and constructive criticism rather than on unilateral decision-making and unquestioning obedience.

This is an extremely difficult relationship to sustain in business and causes considerable stress on both sides. It means, for example, that the boss must be willing to subordinate his own self-esteem to the need for better decisions; that he must have the courage to expose himself to new concepts and techniques; and, above all, that he must be prepared to *listen*, a rare and underestimated managerial art. Such paragons are in short supply and are likely to remain so until the older generation of senior managers has been replaced by the more enlightened products of management education.

The high flier too must learn to give as well as take: many are unquestionably their own worst enemies. They should learn to be more tolerant of those whose abilities are more limited and recognize that they must 'sell themselves' as well as their ideas. They also need to be more sensitive to those emotional and political factors which so often affect decision-making and to accept that facts, like patriotism, are not always enough. Not least—and perhaps this is the hardest lesson of all—they need to be far more aware of the dangers of relying too heavily upon flair and intuition to the exclusion of adequate research and analysis.

This, again, is where the right kind of boss can make a vital contribution. Without pouring cold water upon the high flier's ideas, he will nevertheless probe for evidence that his thinking has been adequate. He will want to know the basic assumptions upon which a proposal is based; he will look for clear statements of objectives, costs and the benefits to be gained; above all, he will seek concrete evidence that the high flier has anticipated the potential problems that may arise if his recommendations are accepted. It takes a really high-calibre boss to supply this kind of coaching input, but this is the only approach which both matures the high flier and unleashes his creativity.

Nevertheless, even if the high flier and his boss are not absolute soul-mates, there are a number of basic pitfalls which ought to be avoided (see Fig. 15.1).

Fig. 15.1 Key points checklist for managing the high flier

DO	DO NOT
1. Regard him as a challenge to your management skills.	1. View him as a threat to your own security.
2. Set him clear objectives and aggressive deadlines.	2. Leave him to guess what he is expected to achieve.
3. Make time to discuss his ideas and suggestions.	3. Always be 'too busy' to see him.
4. Challenge his ideas and be constructively critical.	4. Display indifference or be negative and carping.
5. Treat him as a valued member of your team.	5. Make him constantly aware of your senior status.
6. Be quick to praise him for outstanding achievement.	6. Ignore his achievements (or try to steal the credit).
7. See that his salary increases reflect his extra contribution.	7. Reward him exactly the same as everyone else.
8. Ask for his suggestions and ideas on some of your own work problems.	8. Be excessively secretive or discourage his interest.
9. Nominate him for courses which would assist his development.	9. Deny him opportunities in case he should appear more knowledgeable than you.
10. Request only those reports which you really need.	10. Keep badgering him for reports which you promptly file.

Most of these revolve around the boss's use of his managerial prerogatives—particularly the type of supervision which he personally favours. One thing is certain: not one high flier in a thousand will tolerate the kind of autocratic, 'yours not to reason why', coercive approach which was widely practised in industry until about ten years ago, and which has now been thoroughly discredited by the behavioural scientists. Any manager who still relies upon 'rank-pulling' to get things done is as obsolete as the horse-drawn tram and ought to be recognized for what he is—a downright menace to the prosperity of his company. Nevertheless, even though he will rightly resent any attempt at 'close supervision', the high flier must be intelligently controlled: he cannot expect to opt out entirely from the disciplines which an institution must require of its members. The question is: how can this be done without stifling his initiative and enthusiasm?

The answer—as so often happens in management—is easy to specify but difficult to achieve. There are, after all, two quite separate but equally legitimate interests which have to be reconciled: management's need for 'feedback' on performance and the high flier's need for freedom from bureaucratic interference. Take, for example, the somewhat vexed issue of written reports. Few tasks are more demoralizing to the high flier than having to produce unnecessarily detailed and cumbersome reports which are purely historical and which rarely, if ever, lead to action being taken. For a boss to insist upon frequent reports of this type is tantamount to encouraging the high flier to leave the firm at a fairly early date. If, on the other hand, the boss stipulates that he is interested only in the reporting of key results and the reasons for major deviations from standards, then this is a horse of a very different colour. Most high fliers thrive upon 'reporting by exception' because it clearly stresses personal responsibility and encourages self-control. Instead of being a dreary chore, reporting becomes a creative act which gives them a deeply-satisfying sense of controlling their own destinies.

But the issues involved in 'living with' the high flier range far wider and deeper than written reports: the whole system of rewards and punishments under which managers operate can sometimes be brought into extremely sharp focus. For example, any organization in which age and seniority weigh more heavily than performance has very little hope of retaining its high-talent manpower. Such companies are like graveyards to their high fliers who naturally expect to be rewarded according to their results. It is pointless for these firms to complain about 'disloyalty' and 'job hopping' when their high fliers leave: the remedy, quite clearly, is in their own hands. Yet how many firms which advertise for 'men of vision and initiative' take the trouble to create an environment in which these qualities can thrive? There are still many organizations in the UK in which the administration of salaries is about as scientific as Russian roulette; in which job descriptions and performance appraisals are non-existent; and in which management succession planning is simply a matter of the survival of the thickest. Truly, 'the fault, dear Brutus, lies not in our stars but in ourselves'.

No one suggests that it is easy for organizations to change their attitudes and practices but with the ever-increasing tempo of change in modern industry it is rapidly becoming a question of 'adapt or perish!' And whether we like it or not, Pareto's Law is as valid in business as in any other area of human endeavour—80 per cent of the really worthwhile results are obtained by only 20 per cent of the people employed. The problems involved in managing and developing the high flier are therefore inextricably linked, not merely with the survival of individual firms but with national survival and economic growth.

16

How to develop yourself

During the past decade, formal management development schemes have penetrated almost every sector of British industry. No longer the preserve of a few wealthy companies, they have become an accepted part of the industrial scene, a major item in the drive for greater profitability and more effective management. Spurred on by the demands of the Industrial Training Act, industry has recruited hundreds of training specialists to analyse its needs and to formulate policies and programmes which, it is hoped, will produce the required results.

Management development has become a thriving specialization, with an impressive armoury of techniques and a strange new vocabulary derived from the behavioural sciences. The air is filled with talk of 'T-Groups' and 'Grid plans'; of 'Theory X and Theory Y'; of 'job enrichment' and 'hygiene factors'; of Maslow's 'hierarchy of needs' and Likert's 'System 4'. The results have been predictable. Confronted by so many mysteries, daunted by so much technique, many managers have abdicated their responsibility for their own self-development.

This is a mistake; indeed, a major error of judgement. For just as no manager can escape his responsibility for developing his subordinates, neither can he evade the parallel obligation to develop himself. If he, in effect, 'contracts out' from this responsibility, preferring instead to rely wholly upon the judgement of specialists, he will fail to grasp those countless opportunities for self-improvement which occur spontaneously in the day to day operation of his job. For it is within the job environment with all its pressures and challenges that the most effective development takes place—not in the rarefied atmosphere of the conference room where virtue wins no prizes and mistakes can be made without fear of retribution.

As always, objectives are the starting point. Soberly and without self-deception, the manager should ask himself two searching questions:

1. In what aspects of my current performance do I need to improve?

2. What new knowledge and skills do I need in order to equip myself for promotion?

The majority of large and medium-sized companies now operate formal staff appraisal schemes which provide an invaluable source of feedback upon a manager's performance. But even in companies which do not have such schemes, continual discussions take place between a manager and his boss about performance standards and results achieved. Often the manager is left in no doubt whatever about those areas where improvement is necessary; at other times criticism may be given in a more oblique and subtle way.

The sensible manager does not waste time and energy in resenting such comments. He knows that constructive criticism demands a positive response and that the remedy lies essentially in his own hands. His first step, therefore, will be to produce a list of self-development objectives and then he will consider the various alternative means of achieving them. For example, he may decide to apply for a place on an in-company course which covers precisely those areas of knowledge and skill in which he is deficient; or, if none such exists, he may apply for a relevant external course, having previously discussed his needs with the company training specialist. The essential point is that nothing is likely to happen unless he, the manager, tries to *make* it happen—unless he is prepared to take the initiative in 'breaking the ice' and *to create his own opportunities.* Contrary to the well known proverb, few things come to him who waits. Just as no child can be made to learn, so no manager can be forcibly 'developed' by someone else: he can only develop himself as a result of his own enthusiasms and aspirations.

Let us now consider some of the various ways in which a manager can implement this philosophy of self-development to the benefit of both himself and his company. Naturally, it is not suggested that all of these methods are applicable to all managers or to all situations. It is for the manager to exercise his judgement in selecting those which are most relevant to his personal needs and to the environment in which he works. Nevertheless, it is hoped that readers will be able to detect a certain consistency of purpose in each of these examples—above all, the persistent encouragement of self-help and self-reliance on the part of the manager himself.

Delegation of responsibility

Many managers are ambitious, but too few play a really positive role in preparing themselves for promotion. In considering the job of their superiors, for example, some grossly underestimate the often formidable requirement for additional knowledge and skill which such posts demand. The technical specialist, in particular, is prone to overvalue the importance of sheer technical expertise in a management job and to ignore the much more exacting areas of leadership, administrative ability and financial control. So when promotion does arrive, he finds himself completely out of his depth.

Since all knowledge is derived from experience (either one's own or someone else's), the prudent manager will seize every possible opportunity of exposing himself to problems and situations which will test his capacity to acquire new knowledge and skill. For example, he will actively encourage his boss to delegate more challenging assignments to him—perhaps in the form of a short-term project, such as a special investigation into a long-standing problem which the boss himself has not had the time to undertake.

There is no better way for a manager to prepare himself for possible promotion to his boss's job than by learning about its problems at first hand—and *before* he becomes fully accountable himself. To cope with the extra work load, he will, of course, need to organize his own operation more effectively and to delegate more widely to his own subordinates. The result is that 'on-the-job' training begins to penetrate all levels of management in a totally realistic way. And even when the boss is not a particularly good delegator, he can still be asked questions about his problems—questions which not only demonstrate his subordinate's keenness and interest, but which also encourage him to be somewhat bolder in future in communicating his wisdom and experience.

While no soldier can truly prove his mettle until it has been tested in the heat of battle, it is better that he should have fought even a mock-battle than none at all. Similarly, provided that a manager is reasonably tactful and not overly aggressive in his efforts to gain more insight into his boss's problems, he will, in most cases, find him increasingly willing to delegate and to share his experience. In this way, the manager can enrich his job and develop his potential in that most valuable of all training arenas—his own particular work environment. And, after all, it is very much in the boss's own interest to develop a successor; all too often it is the lack of a suitable replacement which causes him to miss promotion opportunities himself.

Lecturing on training courses

Every company contains within its ranks a large (and often untapped) reservoir of potential teaching ability—its own managers. Much of the disappointment experienced by companies which use external courses as the keystone of their development programmes could be avoided if they were to make greater use of the resources available within their own organizations. Nor does this mean simply abdicating the running of in-company courses to the specialist training staff; it involves a conscious effort to secure the services of managers as teachers and discussion leaders. No one learns more about a subject than he who is required to teach it to others—particularly if the situation requires him to defend his views in open debate.

90

Any manager who is invited to contribute to an in-company course should see it as an opportunity not only to help others but to further his own development (the same applies to invitations to speak on external courses). It provides, after all, a threefold opportunity: to practise his personal communications skills, to project an authoritative image of himself within the company and, hopefully, to garner the occasional new idea or approach to a problem which is troubling him. These are benefits which will handsomely repay the investment of time which such commitments involve.

Discussions with colleagues

Management development is not something which only occurs in classrooms; opportunities can arise in even the most seemingly innocuous situations. A manager's colleagues, in particular, often represent a rich vein of knowledge and experience which can be systematically quarried in order to meet his individual needs. And yet, especially in large organizations, many managers operate as though their departments were bounded by electrified fences and make little effort to get to know their colleagues in other departments or to understand their problems.

The manager who is keen on self-improvement makes no such error. If his need is for more knowledge about computers, then he will make it his business to meet the data processing manager and learn the things he needs to know. Similarly, if his knowledge of finance is weak, he will take—and create— every opportunity he can of discussing his problems with the chief accountant, during lunch in the canteen or even after working hours over a pint in the local pub. Every modern company of any appreciable size consists of a complex network of many different specializations; it is up to the individual manager to 'tap in' on those particular 'nets' which contain the expertise that he requires.

An approach which some companies use to combat the increasingly serious problem of managerial parochialism and isolation is to form a managers' luncheon club which meets, say, once a fortnight, to discuss current company problems which are of general concern to all managers. Sometimes such discussions will be led by a director or a senior corporate specialist. Often, however, a line manager with a particularly pressing problem will be invited to give a succinct presentation of the situation after lunch, followed by a general discussion period in which ideas, no matter how 'impractical', are invited from any quarter. Clearly, this kind of managerial 'brainstorming' can benefit not only the individual with the problem but can also facilitate better communication and understanding within the whole management group. Management development becomes a reality because it is focused on actual company problems which demand solutions.

Professional associations

Vast numbers of managers are also members of professional institutions but only a minority play an active part in their meetings and functions. Any manager who is bent upon self-improvement should participate enthusiastically in the work of his local branch. Not only will he have the opportunity of hearing and discussing expert presentations on some of the latest techniques within his own field; there is also a rich harvest to be gained by discussing common problems with fellow managers from other organizations. Out of such exchanges of ideas and experience many valuable ideas may emerge which he can then apply in the context of his own job. In this way—as happens on any effective training course—managers are essentially teaching themselves and are constantly contributing to each other's development.

Frequently some of the contacts made at these meetings eventually blossom into personal friendships, resulting in regular off-duty meetings to discuss matters of common concern. No manager should neglect the opportunity to build up his own personal network of business contacts. It is, to say the least, extremely useful to be able to discuss one's current problems with other managers who may have faced precisely the same difficulties in the recent past.

Evening classes, correspondence courses

Evening classes and correspondence courses are among the most traditional methods of self-development and have enabled many managers to obtain knowledge and qualifications useful to them in their careers. They can, however, make considerable demands upon a manager's personal life, especially if he is married and has a family, and should not be undertaken without due recognition of the adjustments which may be necessary. Needless to say, any manager whose job involves considerable travel should think carefully before he enrols for evening classes; similarly, if his home does not contain a 'den' or other room suitable for private study, he may well find that his correspondence course—or, rather, his need for peace and quiet—can result in strained relationships within the family circle!

Before embarking upon such studies, therefore, the manager should make absolutely certain that the course will be of value to him in his career. Often the best approach is for him to discuss his plans with the company training officer who can frequently give valuable advice regarding the most suitable courses and institutions; nor should he neglect to seek his boss's views. In short, provided that these preliminary researches have been carried out, correspondence courses and evening classes can play a useful role in a manager's self-development programme. If they are ignored, the result may be a considerable waste of time and a consequent lowering of the manager's morale as he begins to realize that he has 'bitten off more than he can chew'.

Self-analysis

'Know thyself' is an injunction which many pragmatic and outward-looking managers find it difficult to heed. And yet the manager who is constructively introspective, and is keen to evaluate the effect which he has upon other people, will often discover valuable clues to his own self-development needs. As Alan Mumford pointed out:*

> A manager who watches and listens to the reactions of his colleagues to his ideas and proposals may learn that what to him is self-confidence appears to them as arrogance, what to him is caution to them seems to be procrastination, what to him seems natural reserve to them seems unwillingness to respond or what to him is a clever point to them is a clever-clever point.

This kind of self-knowledge can, of course, only be obtained if the manager really *wants* to learn and to improve; those whose vanity (or insecurity?) causes them to be chronically insensitive to their effect upon others will be unwilling to submit themselves to such a potentially painful process of self-examination. But for those who are willing to watch, listen and perceive, there is a rich harvest to be gained in terms of greater managerial effectiveness. To quote an ancient Chinese proverb:

> He who knows others is worldly
> But he who knows himself is wise.

A self-development checklist

The following checklist is offered as an *aide memoire* to any manager who is interested in doing everything possible to develop himself:

1. Do you really want to develop? Are you prepared to make the necessary efforts both on the job and in your own personal time?
2. Do you have clear objectives? What are your main improvement needs in your present job? What job do you hope to be doing in, say, three to five years' time, and what new knowledge, skills and experience will you need to acquire?
3. Have you discussed your needs and plans with your boss and/or the company training specialist?
4. Are you constantly seeking opportunities to acquire new experience in your present job? Do you actively encourage your boss to delegate to you?
5. Are you following a systematic reading programme of books and journals in order to keep up to date with developments both in your own specialist field and in the wider field of general management?

* Mumford, Alan, 'Self development for the manager', *Personnel Management*, January 1972.

6. Do you seek out colleagues within the company who have knowledge and experience which you need and discuss your problems with them?
7. Have you ever applied for a place on an in-company/external training course on a subject which is relevant to your needs? Have you ever volunteered to give a talk on an in-company course?
8. Do you regularly attend the branch meetings of your professional association or institute? Have you ever offered to give a talk or to lead a discussion?
9. Have you investigated the possibility of taking a correspondence course or attending evening classes in a subject which is relevant to your short- or long-term goals?
10. Is there an up-to-date job description for your present job? If not, do you intend to write one and to discuss it with your boss?
11. Have you ever considered the effect which you have upon other people? Have you analysed the improvements which you need to make in your working relationships? Do you really listen to others and watch for their reactions to what you say?
12. Do you constantly encourage your subordinates to develop themselves and do everything possible to help them?

Conclusion

While formal training courses will continue to provide an economic response to many training needs, management development is not simply a matter for training specialists; it is a concern of every manager who seeks fulfilment in his job. And what he learns for himself is likely to make a far greater impact than anything which reaches him at second hand; for it is part of man's nature to prize more highly those things for which he has struggled rather than those which he is given. The self-motivated manager seeks always to control his own destiny, to carve out his own paths; not for him the waiting game since time is short and opportunities fleeting. Such men deserve well. They are, for any company, its best guarantee of survival in a competitive world.

Part 3

What every training professional should know

17

How to plan a manager's development

Company management development schemes too often reflect the values of the conveyor belt rather than those of the master craftsman. Managers are fed into these programmes like components on a vast educational assembly line; quality control is entirely absent; the needs of the individual almost totally ignored. Instead of being an intelligent response to a manager's current or future needs, management training becomes a series of standard inoculations to be taken at prescribed intervals. Small wonder that the victims of these juggernauts are vocal in their criticisms: no manager enjoys being treated like a battery hen.

Effectiveness in management development is related to quality, not quantity: the economies of scale are likely to prove illusory in this sphere. Each manager is an individual who operates within certain finite boundaries of knowledge and skill, authority and responsibility, intelligence and drive. The greater his maturity and experience, the more he will resent a standardized approach to his development—one which takes little account of his feelings and aspirations.

Although the great majority of management development officers are convinced adherents of McGregor's Theory Y, many of them still fail to consult individual managers about their development or to encourage their active participation in development plans. Is it because these are mysteries that only the specialist can unravel? Are the techniques involved so complex as to be incomprehensible to all but the trained professional? Surely not. Most management development techniques present only a modest challenge in purely intellectual terms: the real skill lies in selecting the right combination to meet an individual manager's needs. And however varied these needs may be, the process of satisfying them will involve four basic steps: analysis, selection, control and follow-up.

1. Analysis

This step covers both the definition of objectives and the collection of information about the manager's needs. Often the advice of the management development officer (MDO) will be sought by the manager's superior who will outline the problem as it appears to him. Typically, there will be too much talk about the manager's personality and temperament and all too little about his current and future assignments. The wise MDO will receive such information with diplomatic respect—and inner suspicion. He will know from experience, often bitter, how important it is to check the superior's comments against the evidence of written appraisals, the manager's job description and, not least, the murmurings of his own personal 'grapevine'. When he has done all this, he may feel confident and knowledgeable enough to approach the manager himself.

Hopefully, the latter will be expecting his visit, having already been briefed by his own superior. If not, the MDO should postpone his meeting with the manager until this briefing has taken place—otherwise, he may appear to be offering completely unsolicited comments. But even if the manager has been properly briefed, the MDO should still tread warily, for a discussion on training needs, even when skilfully conducted, can be a delicate undertaking. Most managers have a sizeable investment of ego in their existing practices: the dividing line between offering to help and appearing to threaten is a fine one.

Assuming that the superior has mentioned certain specific needs related either to the manager's current job or to a probable future assignment, the MDO's next task is to determine whether the manager agrees with this assessment. Given a healthy and mature relationship between the man and his boss, disagreement is unlikely. But if the manager does not accept his superior's views, then he may see his meeting with the MDO as an opportunity to 'plead his case', giving a plethora of reasons why his own views are infinitely more balanced and realistic. And, indeed, in some cases, this may be so. Nevertheless, it is not the job of the MDO to decide who is right, but to take effective action in the light of the facts available. This could well involve him in recommending to the man's superior that further action should be postponed until these differences have been resolved—or at least sufficiently modified to make future planning feasible. After all, a manager's performance cannot be improved by diktat; nor can the MDO hope to cope singlehanded with a relationship that has gone sour. These problems must be worked through where they belong—in the normal executive line of command.

2. Selection

Once the needs have been defined and objectives set, it remains to select the right tools and to devise an effective strategy. There is a whole battery of factors which have to be considered: the manager's age, experience and educational background; the current pressures in his job; the availability of both internal and external educational facilities; the man's own enthusiasm and desire to improve. An effective development programme will contain a judicious mixture of company support and individual self-help. Frequently, too much faith is placed in the curative properties of formal courses to the exclusion of systematic attempts to improve performance on the job. For example, how many development plans make a sustained effort to involve *superiors* in the development of their subordinates? And yet there are so many ways in which the superior can contribute: by setting objectives, key tasks and clear-cut standards of performance; by assigning special projects and delegating the necessary authority; and, not least, by seeking his subordinate's views on more complex problems which will challenge his initiative and creative powers.

The manager, too, must be prepared to play his part; there can be no 'spoon-feeding' if he is to be truly stretched. One rewarding approach is for the MDO to devise a planned reading programme for every manager being developed—to assign each man a key 'book of the month', related to his needs, which he will be required to discuss with his superior and his colleagues at a future departmental meeting. There is also much to be gained by encouraging the manager to participate in the activities of professional bodies and associations where he will have the opportunity to exchange ideas and experience with men of similar calibre from other organizations.

In planning the manager's development programme, the MDO will consider what part an appropriate high-quality external course might play in meeting the objectives. But he would do well to recognize the limitations of what is often only a temporary 'shot in the arm', with no lasting effects upon a manager's motivation and performance. If the course has been carefully selected—and if the man's superior accepts that he has a responsibility to help his subordinate to apply his newly-acquired knowledge—then it may indeed prove a sound investment. If not, the effect may be simply to build in frustration and cause the manager's performance to deteriorate rather than improve.

3. Control

Having produced a balanced programme, the MDO should then seek a further discussion with the manager to outline his plans. Some MDOs neglect this step, preferring to deal direct with the man's superior. Unless there are very special reasons for doing so, this is a serious mistake. It leaves the manager with the suspicion that he is being manipulated: that he is of insufficient account to have a voice in his own development. By neglecting this vital consultative step or by delaying it until after his discussion with the superior (when it may appear to the manager that he is being presented with a *fait accompli*), the MDO is risking the success of the entire programme. A manager's participation in plans which affect his development is not a mere optional extra: it is a motivational 'must' if he is to be fully committed and involved.

Discussion of the programme with the manager will often reveal its short-comings and ensure that it is reality-based. Once the manager begins to respond to the challenge of this participative approach—instead of merely sitting back and passively accepting the fate ordained for him—he will be keen to contribute his own ideas and suggestions on how the objectives might best be achieved. This makes it much easier for the MDO to move the discussion gradually into a mutual consideration of how the manager's progress is to be measured and controlled. This, it may be argued, is the superior's job, not the MDO's. Theoretically, this may be so but, in practice, how many busy line executives have either the time or the know-how to construct the kind of formal checkpoints that will enable the subordinate's progress to be effectively monitored?

For example, if the manager is carrying out a planned reading programme as part of his development, it is more than likely that it will fall to the MDO to arrange a meeting with his superior during which any new ideas gleaned from his reading can be discussed and evaluated. Similarly, if he is working on a special project designed to give him the opportunity of acquiring new knowledge and experience, the MDO must be prepared to take the initiative in organizing the necessary progress review meetings. Again, if the manager has attended a course, the suggestion that he should produce a report after his return—or give a short oral presentation at a departmental meeting—will, in many cases, come from the MDO rather than the manager's superior. And rightly so. It is a vital part of the MDO's professional role that he should be capable of structuring situations that will provide the required feedback. Indeed, unless he is willing and able to act as both catalyst and coordinator, the whole impetus of the programme may be lost in that whirlpool of daily job pressures which so often engulfs a manager's attempts to plan and control his work.

Each part of the manager's programme should be critically examined and the necessary control points established. Target dates must be sensible, standards agreed and the manager's personal contribution to his development clearly defined. Bearing in mind that the programme is still only provisional, the views of the manager's superior must now be sought and any necessary adjustments made. Provided that the MDO's initial research into the training needs has been thorough and that his discussions with the manager have been realistic, it is unlikely that his superior will have any major criticisms of the overall strategy. The key point for the MDO to emphasize at this stage is that the boss must be willing to invest some of his own time in the programme: that it is *his* attitudes, *his* enthusiasm, *his* participation which may make all the difference between success or failure.

100

4. Follow up

Control and evaluation of a development programme should be a continuous process and much will depend on the degree of rapport and teamwork that exists between the manager, his superior and the MDO. In the early stages of implementation, the MDO's role is essentially a mixture of 'gadfly' and 'father confessor'. He should be present at all progress reviews between the manager and his superior, not only to assess how effectively the plan is working but also to enable him to decide whether any amendments are required to the later stages of the programme. For example, it may be clear to him after one or two of these early feedback sessions that he has overestimated the manager's capabilities, and that the man is finding it difficult to cope with his development assignments in addition to the normal pressures of his job. If this is the case, then either the manager's future assignments must be modified to make them less exacting or his job must be restructured by his boss to enable him to devote more time to his development plan. Conversely, it may happen that the man has sailed through his early assignments with an ease and panache which suggests that his programme is not sufficiently challenging—in which case it would be necessary to abandon the gradualist approach and to 'telescope' his programme so that each remaining project thoroughly 'stretches' him to the limit of his capabilities. For example, a sales promotion manager whose efforts have hitherto been largely confined to retaining his company's market share in a relatively static market might be charged with the responsibility of developing a complete marketing plan for launching a new product in either a highly competitive or an uninhabited market. The essential point is that the programme should be kept flexible rather than become an end in itself: it must be tailored to the man, not to a rigid timetable which may quickly become unrealistic or out of date. (An abbreviated example of such a programme is shown in Fig. 17.1.)

When the manager has worked through his programme, a period of between three and six months should be allowed for the accumulation of evidence regarding the effect upon his performance. The more experienced the manager, the more time he will need to adjust his attitudes and to implement his new knowledge and skill in the day-to-day operation of his job. Once again, it is vital that the MDO should take action, with the manager's superior, to ensure that he is kept fully informed of the results of the programme, as reflected in the man's performance. Otherwise the MDO's own attitudes may become as outdated and inflexible as those of some of the managers whom he is trying to help.

To summarize: if a manager is to develop successfully, then he is entitled to be consulted about his needs and to play an active role in development planning. Unless he becomes truly committed and involved, no amount of 'technique' or specialist wizardry will kindle his enthusiasm. The MDO, for his part, must constantly work to establish himself with his managerial

Fig. 17.1 Management development plan

A. Personal Details

Name: A. J. Coates. Age: 32. Job title: Market Development Supervisor—A Division.

Responsible to: Divisional Marketing Manager—A Division. Date joined company: 1 March 1968.

Experience in Company: 4½ years as salesman, selling in highly competitive industrial markets. Outstanding sales record—'Salesman of the Year' 1971. Promoted to present job October 1972. No subordinates at present. Responsible for finding and developing new markets for Division's products.

B. Objective

To test his ability to acquire the requisite knowledge, skills and attitudes to justify his promotion to Divisional Marketing Manager by 1 December 1974.

C. Plan

Sept.–Dec. 1973

1. Attends Basic Marketing course at .... on 3–15 November.

2. Carries out Marketing Project A, under general supervision of Divisional Marketing Manager (DMM).

3. Reads selected books on marketing and management (schedule should be attached).

4. Gives presentation on Marketing Project A to DMM and members of marketing group.

Jan.–April 1974

1. Attends in-company Principles of Management course on 14–15 January.

2. Carries out Marketing Project B under general supervision of DMM.

3. Gives presentation on Marketing Project B to DMM and members of marketing group.

4. Discusses new ideas gained from management course/reading programme with DMM and MDO and submits plans for implementation.

May–Aug. 1974

1. Attends Marketing Statistics and Sales Forecasting course at .... on 21–23 May.

2. Prepares Divisional sales forecast under general supervision of Divisional Accountant.

3. Gives presentation of Divisional sales forecast to General Manager, DMM and Divisional Accountant.

Sept.–Dec. 1974

1. Attends Marketing course at .... on 9–13 September.

2. Prepares marketing plan for new product A and discusses with DMM.

3. Organizes and runs two-day Marketing Management Appreciation course for regional managers and supervisors.

colleagues as a fellow contributor to better business results, and not as a mere custodian of theory. This is a reputation that is not easily earned. Participation—not secrecy,—discussion—not manipulation: these are the keys to lasting success.

18

How to involve line managers in training

Any serious talk about management training invariably produces the point that 'training is a line management responsibility'. In too many companies, however, this remains little more than an empty platitude—one which nobody is prepared to contest openly but which few managers take seriously once the meeting is over. And yet the immediate superior at any level in an organization exercises by far the most potent influence, for good or ill, upon the development of his subordinates: by comparison, the impact of formal training courses is relatively peripheral. When an employee returns from a course he re-enters reality—a world in which his boss is the dominant figure. After all, it is he who dispenses rewards and punishments, provides patterns of leadership, creates the 'climate' within the working group and structures the tasks which are necessary to accomplish objectives. For the people whom he controls he *is* 'the company', a living example of management practice whose attitudes and behaviour can enrich or impoverish their working lives.

Yet, even if a manager is conscientious and competent in executing his training responsibilities, many problems and situations will continue to arise where he will recognize the need for specialist advice. Indeed, during the next decade, it is likely that the training officer will become much more of an internal consultant to management and far less of a classroom teacher. 'Conveyor-belt' training courses will be replaced by the kind of organizational development in which the trainer acts as a catalyst and adviser to the working group and is as much respected for his qualities of judgement and insight as for his specialized knowledge of training techniques.

In my own company, we have made a good deal of progress along the road during the past two years and, although much remains to be done, the concept of the corporate training staff as a small group of internal management consultants is now recognized and understood by the majority of our managers. This did not happen overnight: it was a long and gradual process. Nor was it achieved simply by persuading the managing director to authorize a policy statement which was then dutifully imposed upon a sceptical line management. It arose from a conscious determination to involve managers at every stage in the training process and to encourage them to implement their training responsibilities as an integral part of their management of people.

Many books and articles on management development tend to imply that results can be achieved in a totally systematic, step-by-step manner, by first capturing the support of top management and then proceeding through senior and middle management right down to first-line supervision. Unfortunately, as every training officer knows, 'real life' is often very different. For every time that change occurs in the manner described in the textbooks, there are many more occasions when it is a much more erratic and untidy process which owes little to any master-plan. Moreover, in companies with large central training departments, there is a constant temptation for managers to take the line of least resistance and to abdicate their responsibilities to the training specialists. In 3M we believe that there is no substitute for a challenging job—one which fully extends a manager's capabilities and provides him with opportunities to develop himself. It is the boss's responsibility to grasp the opportunities.

The remainder of this chapter will therefore deal with five practical case-histories which will attempt to illustrate how this philosophy is being continually applied in our company in order to give 'teeth' and meaning to our belief in the critical importance of the manager's training role. Naturally, within the confines of a short chapter it is not possible to report these cases in the kind of blow-by-blow detail to be found in the typical Harvard study: by comparison, these are merely vignettes. Nevertheless, it is hoped that readers will be able to detect a certain consistency of purpose in each of these examples—above all, the persistent encouragement of self-help and self-reliance on the part of the managers concerned.

Case no. 1: communications

About eighteen months ago, in spite of an excellent past record of profitability and growth, salesman morale in one of our product groups began to fall somewhat below its customary high standard. This was due largely to short-term distribution problems which had caused difficulties in relationships with customers. Management had acted swiftly to remedy the technical aspects of the problem but had neglected to keep the sales force fully informed of the steps which had been taken.

Predictably, at departmental management meetings attended by the training adviser, the usual cry for 'more training' was heard, notwithstanding the fact that no one seemed able to define precisely just what kind of effort was needed. As often happens in such cases, the executives concerned were tending to look to the training man for a quick panacea which would magically solve the problem with minimum disruption to their normal activities.

However, instead of yielding to these pressures for 'instant training', the training adviser recommended that a series of meetings should be held in each major sales region throughout the UK, at which management would give comprehensive details to the sales forces of the various plans and programmes which had been initiated. These meetings were duly held and the resultant frank interchange of ideas and information quickly restored morale to its former level and rebuilt confidence within the group.

Case no. 2: job descriptions

Although job descriptions had existed for many years, they were designed primarily for job evaluation purposes, and were little used by line managers. The training adviser was therefore assigned by top management to develop a new type of description which would clearly reflect the influence of other current in-company developments in the field of MbO and performance appraisal. A prototype of the new description was then 'test-marketed' by the training adviser who, as a result of discussions with the job holders, produced a number of senior management job descriptions. Even before the new-style job description had been officially launched at our annual senior management conference, several managers—especially those who had been concerned in the pilot study—requested the training adviser to produce further descriptions for those jobs within their departments which had not been written during the initial project.

These requests were politely but firmly refused. Instead, a variety of techniques were employed to ensure that those managers who were interested would receive sufficient instruction and practice to enable them to write their own descriptions for subsequent discussion with, and approval by, their immediate superiors. Training meetings were organized in which practice writing sessions were held; coaching interviews were arranged with individual managers; and a concise explanatory booklet outlining the principles and purposes of job description, with a section on writing techniques, was prepared for general distribution to management.

After the official launching of the new scheme, requests for assistance in writing job descriptions continued to be received in ever-increasing numbers: all were dealt with in the same way. Moreover, there has been no evidence whatever of any resentment on the part of managers at being deprived of the 'spoon-feeding' type of staff support which so many tend to expect in large organizations. On the contrary, the vast majority have expressed considerable enthusiasm for this do-it-yourself approach in which they have been committed and involved from the beginning.

Case no. 3: counselling

Each month, the training adviser conducts many interviews with managers who seek his advice on problems connected with the performance of their subordinates. Invariably, when this service was first established, some managers tended to regard him as a kind of witch-doctor who could instantly transform the behaviour of even the most recalcitrant individual. Many proved to have wildly optimistic expectations of the benefits to be derived from formal training courses: a few seemed totally unaware that they themselves had a key role to play in the development of their staff.

Sometimes, it was true, classroom training had a perfectly valid contribution to make to the solution of a particular individual's training problems, especially where these involved relatively straightforward inputs of knowledge and skill which could be immediately applied on the job. But it was in the much more difficult—and nebulous—area of attitude-change that it frequently became clear that it was the attitudes of the manager himself which needed to change before any real progress could be expected of his subordinates.

The training adviser's strategy, therefore, essentially involved an attempt to divert the manager's gaze away from the enticing vistas of external courses towards an in-depth examination of his own style of management and methods of organization. This is the sort of delicate undertaking that requires a supportive rather than a critical approach if the cooperation of the manager is to be obtained. In the majority of cases, carefully-phrased inquiries about such areas as objective-setting, methods of decision-making, job descriptions and personal coaching rarely failed to increase the manager's awareness of the importance of his contribution. Once again, we have found that most managers react responsibly to this approach and diligently follow up the recommendations which are made.

Case no. 4: induction training

Like most large organizations, our company ensures that new employees attend appropriate induction courses within their first few weeks of service. About a year ago, however, the rapid expansion of our marketing groups resulted in the recruitment of a considerable number of junior marketing executives (we call them 'marketing coordinators') for whom no adequate induction programme existed.

The senior marketing managers' council therefore requested the training adviser to organize such a programme; he, in turn, asked for the assistance of two members of the council in selecting the topics which would be most relevant to the needs of the course members. This team effort resulted in an intensive three-day programme which had as its key objective the provision of adequate knowledge and understanding in the following main areas:

1. The structure, organization and scale of the company's operations, both in the UK and world-wide;
2. The role of the divisional marketing groups and, in particular, the co-ordinating role of the marketing services group;
3. The relevant company policies and procedures relating to the marketing coordinator's job.

Twenty-three members of senior and middle management participated in the final programme, either as speakers or as chairmen, and in all cases the utmost cooperation was received. While the training adviser accepted full responsibility for producing the course timetable and for providing the necessary administrative support, he did not play any significant part in running the course, apart from making a brief introductory presentation on the course objectives and the administrative arrangements.

Here again, the do-it-yourself approach proved very successful and at no time was it suggested that the training adviser should have taken a more prominent role in running the course. The managers concerned accepted their various assignments as legitimate demands upon their time and, in the great majority of cases, enjoyed the opportunity of passing on their specialized knowledge and experience.

Case no. 5: performance appraisal

As a result of developments initiated by our European personnel organization in Brussels, a new performance appraisal scheme was recently launched in the UK company. Unlike its predecessor, the new appraisal form is almost wholly concerned with the measurement of performance and results against agreed standards: personality factors, though not ignored, have lost much of their former significance in the overall appraisal.

During the preliminary planning discussions on the design and content of the new form, it seemed to the UK training adviser that here was a golden opportunity to underline still further the vital importance of the line manager's training role. It was therefore agreed, at his suggestion, that the training and development section of the form should consist of three simple, but searching, questions to the appraiser:

1. What action do *you* propose to take in order to develop this employee?
2. What action has the *employee* agreed to take in order to develop himself?
3. What action, if any, do you recommend should be taken by the *personnel department*?

The sequence of the questions is important. First, a manager is required to examine his own resources in relation to an individual's training needs—not to think automatically in terms of a formal course. For example, it might well be that further delegation of responsibility or the assignment of a special project could have a far greater impact upon an individual's performance than any amount of classroom training. Second, the appraiser is encouraged to make it clear to the employee that he has a duty to develop himself—that he cannot expect to be 'spoon-fed' by either the company or his superior. This emphasis upon self-help could result, for example, in the employee agreeing to undertake a planned reading programme or a course of evening classes in his own time. It is only after a thorough examination of the resources which are available to him as a manager to develop his subordinates that the appraiser is expected to seek the help of the personnel and training specialist.

The moral

The company has still some distance to travel before it can truthfully claim that training is universally accepted as an integral part of every manager's job. But the old parrot-cries of two years ago for 'more courses'—as though they were the sole remedy for every conceivable kind of training need—are now only to be heard infrequently. Perhaps the moral for perceptive training officers is simply this: *do for others only those things which they cannot reasonably be expected to do for themselves.* Be at all times helpful, understanding and resourceful. Give freely of your time and expertise when, for example, you are requested by management to carry out research or to provide the administrative back-up for an important company conference. But recognize that it is in your managerial role as an adviser and counsellor that your most significant contribution to management effectiveness is made—not in your operational role as a runner of courses, however valuable and necessary these may sometimes be.

19

How to become a better speaker

Clearly, it is essential for trainers to be able to speak effectively. But, important though the job requirement is, effective speaking—being able to capture and retain attention and to influence the thinking of other people—has two additional major benefits. Both are closely related to the development of a trainer's potential.

First, no trainer can hope to communicate effectively unless he thinks clearly—unless he has a clear understanding of his objectives, of his audience's needs (whether it consists of a few people or many) and how best to organize the information which will meet those needs. Effective speaking *demands* clear thinking. Second, it can be regarded as a challenge to, and, to some extent, a measurement of, a man's leadership abilities. For if we accept that the essence of leadership in industry is the ability to persuade rather than to coerce, then the connection between effective speaking and the development of a trainer's leadership potential becomes clear. If he can speak effectively, people look up to him, they are influenced by him, he commands their respect. In short, they are acknowledging his *leadership qualities*.

Key problems

What are some of the key problems in speaking and how can they be overcome? Theoretically, a trainer should find speaking easy—much easier, for example, than writing reports. Why? Because when he speaks, he can be much more flexible than when he writes; he has many more powerful weapons at his command.

For example, when speaking, he can:

1. Vary the speed of his delivery, sometimes speaking slowly and sometimes fast;

2. Alter the volume and pitch of his voice to add interest and variety or to emphasize a key point;

110

3. Stop speaking and pause for a few moments to allow a point to sink home;
4. Use gestures, naturally and spontaneously, to convey enthusiasm and conviction.

Compared with when he writes, a trainer enjoys far greater freedom of expression. When writing, he has only a piece of paper on which he inscribes symbols; and he must rely entirely upon punctuation to add emphasis and variety to his thoughts. These just do not compare with the far more potent aids which are available to him when he speaks. Nevertheless, many trainers do find speaking difficult, so let us examine some of the more familiar problems.

Fear of audience. One of the biggest problems is undoubtedly nervous fear of the group—the feeling that he is going to make a fool of himself, that some disaster may strike that will result in grave personal embarrassment and perhaps even ridicule. This gloomy view, though understandable, is both irrational and self-deluding. The truth is that it is totally in the interest of every group to hear a good presentation; no one likes to be bored or confused. After all, to have to listen to a badly-prepared, badly-delivered talk is one of the most painful experiences that life has to offer. The group, no less than the speaker, has a stake in his success.

Nervousness often manifests itself in physical terms—'butterflies' in the tummy, hot and cold flushes, perspiring hands and other disquieting symptoms. The remedy for a trainer faced with such problems lies in taking a positive attitude and in recognizing that this is simply nature's way of signalling to him that he is keyed up to produce an effective performance; that he is in peak condition to make a resounding impact. If, however, he has failed to prepare his material properly, hoping that the inspiration of the moment will carry him through, then he deserves to be nervous and to sink without trace. But if he has prepared effectively, there is no reason for him to be despondent. His nervousness will soon disappear as he becomes immersed in his subject and begins to transmit his enthusiasm and sincerity.

Presentation fears. Many trainers worry about the things that may go wrong when they are giving a presentation. 'What if my mind goes blank and I forget my point?' 'What if I dry up?' If such misfortunes do occur while you are speaking the golden rule is simply this: do not panic and, above all, *do not draw attention to your plight.* Do not, for example, stammer apologetically or mutter feebly about having forgotten your point. *Stop speaking,* look at your notes and either pick up your thread from there or move on to your next point. What's done is done—get back into your stride as quickly as possible. There is no need to worry about the group in such situations: they are sympathizing with you, not sneering at you. Most of them are thinking 'there but for the grace of God go I', and are wondering what *they* would do if it had happened to them. They are living out the situation with you and hoping that you will get back on course as quickly as possible. No man is an island when such problems occur.

The seven key areas

Basically, there are seven key areas in effective speaking. They are:

1. The introduction.
2. Use of the voice.
3. Choice of words.
4. Audience contact.
5. Verbal and visual aids.
6. Mannerisms.
7. The conclusion.

The remainder of this chapter deals with each of these aspects, briefly, in turn.

1. **The introduction.** This is very important—first impressions are often critical. Keep your introductory remarks as brief and succinct as possible. Do not plough through some laborious anecdote which most of the group has probably already heard. Instead, state your objectives and how you propose to achieve them—what your main headings are or what questions you propose to answer. Be businesslike: set the right tone from the start.

2. **Use of the voice.** Your volume must be adequate at all times. Keep your head well up so that the sound is directed at the audience, not at the table. As a general rule, speak a shade louder than you might at first consider necessary. Time after time I have been told by trainers on speaking courses that they were convinced that they had been speaking loudly during their presentations —when in fact they could hardly be heard at the back of the room.

Second, try to use your voice *interestingly*. The voice is the musical instrument of the human body and yet so often a talk is delivered in a dull, repetitive monotone, with no light and shade whatsoever. Frequently the speaker is the most natural and friendly of men and is easy to listen to during normal conversation, but these qualities desert him when he gets to his feet. Be natural, not inhibited: do not be afraid to show your enthusiasm by bringing some variety and colour into your tone. Unless you have the ability to 'project' your personality, your views, however well-reasoned, may fail to carry conviction.

Equally important is the question of the *speed* at which you speak. What you have to achieve is a sensible balance between the twin extremes of

(a) speaking so slowly that people begin to day-dream,

and

(b) speaking so quickly that they cannot possibly keep up with you.

112

In both cases, the result is the same: loss of interest and increasing boredom. Once again, aim at variety. Vary your pace, sometimes speeding up when dealing with background material, slowing down when you are making a major point. And remember that often the most effective action you can take after having made such a point is to *pause* for a few seconds to let its full impact register.

3. Choice of words. Use simple, natural words—the kind you use all the time in less formal situations. Assess realistically what the group can be expected to know about your subject and choose the words which they will find most easy to understand. Avoid using, without adequate explanation, behavioural science 'jargon' or specialist training terms. While a group is impressed by clarity, it is irritated by obscurity.

4. Audience contact. This simply means that, if you want to make an impact on your audience, you must look at *them*—not at the table, the floor, the ceiling or the window. Talking to small groups presents few problems; speaking to large numbers means that you must mentally divide your audience into sections and look at each group in turn. It is vital that you distribute your audience contact fairly. Too many trainers address all their remarks to a few individuals or to a particular section of the group, thereby causing no little resentment on the part of those whom they ignore.

5. Verbal and visual aids. Visual aids can serve a most useful purpose when they are skilfully used. But do not become hypnotized by them—too many visuals can be irritating and boring. Use them to make a point or an impact which could not be better made in any other way; be selective and discriminating. And when a visual has served its purpose, remove or conceal it immediately. If you leave it exposed after it has made its point, it will distract the group's attention from what you are saying. Let the visual *aid* you, not compete with you.

You can also use words to paint a word-picture of the situation which you are describing. Give real-life examples to illustrate your points with names, dates, places and other descriptive material. The group will find your material much easier to follow and infinitely more interesting.

6. Mannerisms. Many trainers have highly distracting mannerisms—tricks of speech or particular physical movements which often tend to irritate a group. Usually they are completely unaware of their mannerisms; not so their audiences. And when a mannerism is particularly annoying or fascinating, many course members will actually begin to count the number of times it occurs—be it how many times the trainer takes off his spectacles, puts them on again, smoothes back his hair or fiddles with some object on the table in front of him.

113

Frankly, a trainer with highly distracting physical mannerisms needs expert attention on an advanced speaking course for real progress to be made. But many verbal mannerisms can be detected by listening to oneself on tape—listening really objectively as though hearing a stranger—and noting any words or phrases which are tending to be over-used.

7. The conclusion. How do you 'finish off'? The simplest and easiest method is to summarize the main points which you have made, or, alternatively, to recapitulate the headings or questions which you outlined at the beginning of the talk. Often, too, this is the moment when you may wish to pose a provocative question to spark off the subsequent discussion; or you may decide to round off your talk with an apt quotation. Needless to say, if you use a quotation, make sure that you use it accurately and that it is relevant to your theme.

One final point: if you wish to be able to speak more effectively, then learn to *know yourself*. Public speaking is a revealing process. It reveals what kind of man you are, how you think, the things that matter to you, your values and your prejudices—in short, what 'makes you tick'. And the better you know yourself, the more that you can develop the ability to see yourself as others see you, the more likely it is that you will be able to present your thoughts in a way that will compel attention and command respect.

20

How to run more effective courses

For many training officers, in-company courses are a cross to be borne rather than an opportunity to be grasped—an unwelcome diversion from more interesting tasks, such as counselling managers on their individual needs. Yet, if properly planned and conducted, such meetings can make an effective contribution to better performance.

Courses are notoriously expensive and those who convene them bear a heavy responsibility to ensure that the time and cost are justified by the results. Yet meetings are often organized to discuss topics which concern only a minority of managers in the company: the time of the other course members is grossly misused and the meeting ends in an atmosphere of resentment and frustration.

Before organizing a course, a trainer should ask himself four searching questions:

1. What is my objective—what do I hope to achieve?
2. Is a course necessary—could I achieve my objective in some other way?
3. Is it worth the cost?
4. Who should attend—who needs the knowledge and skills which will be covered on the course?

Courses can serve a variety of purposes. Some are called simply to pass on information about new management techniques. Other typical subjects include management principles, communications skills and 'brain-storming' for new or creative ideas. Whatever the subject, the course has little hope of being effective unless the trainer is clear about why it is necessary and what benefits he believes the course members will obtain.

Some other crucial factors in course management are treated below.

1. **Planning.** Assuming that the course is needed, it is not sufficient for the trainer merely to give the course members a few days' notice and hope that their commitments will permit them to attend. Except in emergencies,

115

managers will resent being summoned from their tasks virtually without warning, with all the disruption to their plans which this often entails. The trainer should give as much notice as possible if the course does not already form part of a well-published schedule. A short note or circular setting out the time and place of the course and including a brief agenda of the topics to be covered will ensure not only that members have an opportunity to plan their work; it will also enable them to think about the problems involved and to prepare some possible contributions. The quality of their thinking is also likely to be much more mature than if they are placed in a situation requiring 'instant thought', with its built-in hazards of shallowness and superficiality.

2. **Continuity.** Many courses suffer disastrously from interruptions, particularly from incessant telephone calls. The trainer must make up his mind just what interruptions, if any, he is prepared to tolerate and take action to keep them within these limits: he cannot hope to run an effective meeting and continue 'business as usual' at the same time. A notice affixed to the door of the conference room will effectively protect him against unscheduled visitors. Similarly, telephone calls can be intercepted by his secretary who should be instructed to put through only those of the highest priority. Foreseeing and dealing with possible interruptions is an indispensable part of effective planning and does much to ensure that discussions are not constantly sidetracked and valuable contributions subsequently overlooked.

3. **General approach.** There are two main approaches to running training courses: the *directive* and the *permissive*. According to advocates of the directive approach, the trainer's prime responsibility is to provide forceful leadership, which in practice means keeping a tight rein over the discussion and displaying an almost aggressive concern for the relevance of members' contributions. Often, such a trainer will have decided in advance those aspects of the subject which he wishes to be discussed and will be somewhat inflexible in his reaction to items which do not fit in with his preconceived plan. The atmosphere at such meetings is one of discipline, order—and tension. Course members display little humour and tend to communicate in a guarded rather than an open manner.

The permissive approach is based upon the premise that men are more likely to commit themselves to the achievement of goals which they have been allowed to participate in setting: that creativity is best ignited when individuals feel free to contribute in an atmosphere of mutual respect. This does *not* mean that the 'permissive' trainer allows anarchy to flourish at his meetings: it *does* mean that he recognizes that the best results are obtained when the course members are willing to control themselves. Like all worthwhile objectives, this is easier to state than to achieve and the trainer may encounter many initial setbacks before the final breakthrough. What steps can he take in order to achieve increased commitment, higher involvement and better results?

4. Making a good start. The manner in which the trainer opens the meeting is crucial: first impressions are often lasting ones. The purpose of the course should be defined and the amount of time available for discussion made clear. This is not 'steam-rollering': the group will not thank a trainer for permitting lengthy discussion of a topic which later turns out to be totally irrelevant. Effective discussion can only take place when the boundaries, if any, have been clearly defined.

5. Handling the discussion. Some trainers insist that every point made should 'go through the chair': the result is a boring succession of dialogues between individual speakers and the trainer. If course members are to be encouraged to generate and exchange ideas, protocol must be kept to a minimum. The wise trainer constantly tries to broaden the discussion by 'tapping' the know-ledge and experience present in the group and encouraging a healthy cross-fertilization of ideas. This does not mean that he remains entirely passive and merely 'holds the ring'. From time to time he will contribute his own views and comments, but in a manner which makes it plain that he expects them to be discussed as objectively and incisively as those of any other member, and is not trying to coerce the meeting by virtue of his position. Nevertheless, he will not contribute too frequently. At this stage of the meeting his job is to act as a catalyst and to ensure that all shades of opinion have an equal opportunity to be expressed. He is group-centred rather than authority-centred, participative rather than dominant, a team member rather than an autocrat.

6. Irrelevance. Even the best-run courses encounter the problem of irrele-vance—the well-meant contribution which sidetracks the discussion and wastes valuable time. It is a situation which provides a stern test for the 'permissive' trainer. The easiest—and least intelligent—course is simply to 'squash' the offender with a curt reminder about the need to 'keep to the point'. Not surprisingly, he will then proceed to 'withdraw' psychologically from the meeting and is most unlikely to make any further effective contribution. Worse still, the rough handling which he has received may well inhibit the other members from contributing freely and openly. Resentment takes the place of cooperation and the trainer may find himself delivering a monologue rather than running a discussion. This is a high and quite unnecessary price for a trainer to pay for a deficiency in his human relations skills. If the discussion goes off the point, he should intervene tactfully, and either sum-marize the discussion up to the stage at which it began to digress or raise a new aspect of the subject for the course members to consider. With tolerance and persistence, these tactics will generate a greater concern for relevance among

117

the members themselves so that control comes from within the group instead of being imposed externally by the trainer. For a course leader to have to ostracize or humiliate a member in order to retain control of the meeting is an admission of defeat.

7. Taking sides. Sometimes a trainer may be tempted, or even invited, to take sides during a meeting: to pronounce for or against a particular point of view. Once again, it is all too easy to destroy the creative spirit of a course by tactless handling of what is undoubtedly a delicate situation. Whatever his immediate choice of tactics may be, the guiding principle for the trainer to follow—and to demonstrate—is that he is not for or against *people*: he is for or against *arguments*. By the manner in which he handles the situation he should make it clear that he is concerned only with the rationality and objectivity of the views expressed—not with his personal feelings towards individuals. At all times he should remain impartial in his treatment of members, avoid protracted arguments and be ever ready to throw back controversial points to the meeting. He should not attempt to gag critical or unpopular views but should remain constantly alert for opportunities to get agreement. Frequently, the emotional temperature of a meeting can be reduced by the trainer's intervention with a timely summary of what has been agreed so far, thus focusing the group's attention on their achievements as a spur to further progress.

8. Ending effectively. Just as some salesmen fail at the point of closing a sale, so some trainers fail to close their courses effectively. An invigorating discussion may be wasted because the meeting runs out of time and breaks up before any definite conclusions have been reached. This is nearly always due to poor leadership and control by the trainer and, specifically, to his failure to use his most powerful and constructive tool: the summary. As each main topic of the course is discussed, the trainer, as stated previously, should remain constantly watchful for the emergence of views and opinions which appear to be generally endorsed. If he has not already voiced his reservations, he should now proceed to do so. If, however, he agrees, then he should crisply summarize the agreed conclusions, and assign any follow-up work to be done by the course members when they return to their jobs. He can then close the course, confident that each member knows what has been decided and what is expected of him. The more that the trainer uses this technique, the more likely it is that effective action will result from the course, thus justifying the time and expense involved.

Provided that they are well planned and skilfully controlled, there is no reason why training courses should be so often associated with frustration and apathy rather than with creativity and teamwork. In his role as course leader, the trainer must effectively blend the decisiveness of the general with the subtleties of the psychologist and this, admittedly, is no easy task. It can only be achieved by trainers who are mature enough to regard course members as their key resource and who are willing, in Peter Drucker's phrase, 'to build on strengths'. For the trainer who persists in his determination to run more effective training courses, the rewards are great: more highly motivated course members, greater respect for his leadership and, most important, improved performance and better results. This is surely a challenge which is worth accepting.

21

How to select external speakers

Sooner or later, most training officers who operate in the management and supervisory fields are faced with the problem of selecting or recommending a guest speaker for an in-company course or conference. Very often, such presentations are regarded as the highlight of the course and can exert a make-or-break influence upon its success or failure. All too frequently, however, speakers are selected haphazardly and are thrust into the arena with only the flimsiest of briefings. As a result, their contributions lack both relevance and impact and, in the atmosphere of recrimination which invariably follows such setbacks, management's confidence in the training officer's judgement can be seriously impaired.

As in all training activities, success in this area requires a systematic approach, based upon a penetrating analysis of the key performance needs. This chapter will therefore discuss such an approach, using as a framework a practical five-step plan.

1. Define the objectives

The training officer's first and most important task is to decide whether the use of an outside speaker can be justified. Such a decision must be taken on rational, not emotional grounds. It is not sufficient, for example, to assume that the course members will inevitably benefit from seeing a fresh face or that every outside speaker is pulsating with new ideas which are bound to be of interest. Few experiences are more annoying to course members than to be harangued by so-called experts, whose knowledge and experience are no greater—indeed, are often less—than their own.

The only valid reason for using an outside speaker is the belief that he will do a better job on his particular subject than anyone else from within the company. Right from the start the training officer should spell out the specific results and benefits which he expects the presentation to achieve. Clearly, such expectations must be realistic, since not even the most practised speaker can hope to perform miracles in the short time which is normally available to him. His prospects of success will be much greater if his presentation is planned, not as a diversion, but as an integral part of the course. For example, he can be used either to introduce a major new topic or as a perceptive and authoritative commentator on ground which has already been covered. In either case, he will be seen by the course members as having a worthwhile contribution to make: one which fits in logically with the overall objective of the course.

2. Select the speaker

A really competent speaker has three outstanding characteristics: he knows his subject, he is a skilled communicator and he can stand up to the hurly-burly of questions and discussion. Before making his final choice, the training officer would do well to satisfy himself on all three criteria. The fact that a man has written a book on his subject, or has impressive academic qualifications, is no guide to his powers as a speaker. Nor can it safely be assumed that because a man is a professional lecturer he will be effective in dealing with comments and questions from the course members. Such speakers, especially academics, are used to dealing mainly with relatively passive or captive audiences and can easily be upset by the tough, probing questioning of a lively industrial group. Finally, few groups are likely to be tolerant of any major deficiencies in speaking skills, particularly if they contain members from such functions as sales and marketing whose own standards of competence may be well above average.

3. Brief the speaker

This is a critical step: to neglect it is to invite total failure. A speaker who has been inadequately briefed is like a rifleman firing at an unseen enemy: most of his bullets will miss the mark: if they do strike home, it will be more by luck than judgement. The training officer must therefore act as the eyes of the speaker, guiding him skilfully towards his objective and alerting him to any pitfalls which may lie in his path.

In practical terms, this means that the speaker must clearly understand:

What is expected of him;
How his contribution fits into the objectives of the course;
Who he will be addressing, in terms of the numbers, levels, experience, age range involved;
What, if anything, the group already knows about the subject;
Which topics are likely to be of greatest, or least, relevance and interest;
How much time is available for the presentation.

Armed with the answers to these questions, the speaker will be able to tailor his material to the needs of the group: without such guidance it is probable that he will fail to make an impact. A really professional speaker will want to do his homework anyway, but it is part of the training officer's responsibilities to ensure that he does it. Often a speaker assumes that a presentation which has served him well on previous occasions will be equally valid whatever the circumstances. As a result, he gives an off-the-shelf presentation, which turns out to be totally unsuitable to the needs of the group. If a speaker is reluctant to adapt his material to the requirements of the situation, then this is a clear warning to the training officer that he has selected the wrong man. It is better to break off negotiations at this stage than to yield to pressures which will result in almost certain failure.

Fortunately, there are a number of ways in which the speaker's abilities can be checked. The Management Courses Index will supply reports on speakers to accredited members of its subscriber companies: these reports are factual, informative and can be supplied either by telephone or in writing. A similar service is provided by the BIM through its management education information unit, except that reports are made by telephone instead of in writing. Friends and contacts in other companies are yet another sensible source of information. In the final analysis, however, there is no real substitute for a personal discussion between the training officer and the speaker. Each company has its own particular personality and it is vital that the speaker should be the kind of person who is likely to gain acceptance. No matter how well qualified and experienced he may be, he will be judged largely in terms of his ability to sell his ideas. Empathy, not erudition, is the primary requirement.

4. Agree on administrative details

As every experienced training officer knows, it is easy for a presentation to be ruined by deficiencies in the administrative arrangements. To give one example, even the most experienced speaker will find it hard to retain his grip upon an audience in a room which is too stuffy, or too cold, or too noisy. It goes without saying, too, that the audience's concentration cannot be expected to withstand such interruptions as telephone calls in the conference room or the appearance of attractive secretaries bearing messages for members of the course.

Perhaps the most important issue which the training officer must settle with the speaker is the format of the presentation. For example, does the speaker propose to give his talk and then take questions and discussion, or is he willing to be interrupted at any time? Much will depend upon the amount of time available, quite apart from the natural inclinations of the speaker. A free-rein type of presentation which permits questions and discussion at any time is undoubtedly more popular with course members and tends to generate a livelier atmosphere: on the other hand, it requires considerable skill on the part of the speaker or chairman to prevent the session from being wrecked by the constant raising of red herrings and other irrelevancies. A set-piece presentation, with questions and discussion following the talk, is far more manageable and is less likely to cause problems with the course timetable. It does, however, demand a speaker of high quality, who can retain an audience's attention for long periods without their becoming restive due to the lack of participation. Whichever strategy is decided upon, it is imperative that the course members are informed right at the beginning of the presentation so as to avoid any possible misunderstandings. This can be done either by the training officer, if he is acting as chairman, or by the speaker himself.

5. Evaluate the presentation

Trying to evaluate the impact made by a presentation is a notoriously difficult task: appearances can be extremely deceptive. True, it requires no special expertise to identify the outstanding triumph or the downright catastrophe, but these are comparatively rare occurrences: the vast majority of presentations fit in somewhere between these two extremes.

A technique which is favoured by many training officers is to hold an end-of-course appraisal session, during which members are encouraged to voice their feelings about any of the various elements of the course. While these can undoubtedly be useful, it must be remembered that such sessions often tend to be dominated by an articulate minority who may not represent the general opinion. Another drawback is that some course members, not wishing to appear unduly critical, tend to pull their punches and give an over-polite version of their true feelings.

Experience seems to indicate that it is generally preferable for the training officer to allow a few days to pass by before attempting a serious evaluation. After a week or so, the members are likely to be much more objective and analytical in their assessments, whether these are sought during a personal discussion or by means of a short questionnaire. Basically, there are five key questions which need to be answered:

1. Was the presentation relevant to the objectives of the course?
2. Did it achieve its objective, as stated by the speaker or chairman?
3. If not, why not?
4. If it did achieve it, how do you feel that you benefited personally?
5. If you did benefit, what are your plans for applying what you learned?

Finally, the question arises as to whether it is desirable for the training officer to report back to the speaker on how his presentation was received. My own experience has been that most professionals welcome such feedback which, should they be invited to speak on future courses, enables them to tailor their presentations even more closely to the requirements of the situation. It is generally the poorer performers who tend to adopt defensive or inflexible attitudes and these, in any case, would be unlikely to be invited again.

Conclusion

When selecting a visiting speaker for an in-company course, the wise training officer is neither dazzled by reputation nor hamstrung by personal diffidence. It is his responsibility as the buyer in the situation to ensure that his company obtains value for money. He can be sure of achieving this objective only if he works to a systematic plan, which enables him to maintain overall direction and control. For him to assume that it will be all right on the night is to provide hostages to fortune which are totally unnecessary. Planning, not abdication, is the key to success.

22

How to present a proposal for change

To be successful in his job, a training officer requires not only the ability to analyse problems and determine solutions: he must also be able to sell his ideas effectively to the managers, supervisors and operators who constitute his customers. In the jargon of the behavioural scientist, he is a *change agent*, a man whose *raison d'être* is to bring new thinking to bear upon current problems and opportunities within the organization. Just as the salesman sells products or services, so the training officer sells ideas and concepts which, it is hoped, will result in more effective use of the company's human resources, thereby contributing both to short-term profitability and long-term growth.

Unlike the salesman, however, he is rarely able to demonstrate the proven ability of his product to meet the customer's requirements. Ideas are not like vacuum cleaners: they cannot be operated by merely flicking a switch. Not even the most relevant solution will produce results unless the potential user is motivated to apply it consistently and enthusiastically. It follows, therefore, that the selling of intangibles requires communication and leadership skills of a particularly high order, since successful applications depend more upon the attitudes of the customer than upon the intrinsic merits of the ideas themselves.

To be an articulate and enthusiastic salesman, however, is not enough. The training officer must also marshall his ideas logically and systematically so that they form the kind of spearhead which is capable of penetrating even the most prejudiced opposition. Unpalatable though it may be to him, he should recognize that professional expertise alone is rarely sufficient to overcome the encrusted attitudes of those for whom change may be an unwanted orphan rather than a welcome guest. The most critical factor in determining his success is whether or not his own attitudes to selling are correct and realistic—whether he can show awareness and understanding of his customers' problems and anticipate their predictable reactions to his proposed solutions. Such attitudes must be reflected in reasoned arguments leading to practical recommendations which, in turn, inspire confidence and enthusiasm. Displays of specialist pyrotechnics will result only in boredom and confusion.

Let us now examine an effective selling strategy for the training officer who is faced with the task of influencing a meeting to accept a proposal for change. Whatever his specific objective, whether it be to bring about a change of policy or procedure, method or attitude, there are five key questions which he must seek to answer—questions which each member of the meeting will have uppermost in his mind. They are as follows:

1. What is the proposal?
2. What is wrong with the present situation?
3. How will the proposed solution work?
4. How much will it cost?
5. What are the advantages?

Each of these questions must be answered clearly and systematically. The remainder of this chapter will show how this can be achieved within the framework of a logical five-step plan—one which I have used for many years in the training of training officers and which has consistently produced encouraging results.

Step 1. State your objective and outline your proposal. A clear and succinct beginning to your presentation is absolutely vital; any confusion at this stage may cause the majority of the audience to lose all further interest. State your objective in precise, down-to-earth language which leaves no possible scope for misinterpretation—never use vague or woolly phrases which result in ambiguity. Next, state your proposal, clearly and specifically, but without giving too much detail at this stage: it is far too early yet to plunge into the nuts and bolts of your proposed solution.

Avoid at all costs the kind of rambling opening statement which rapidly generates boredom and impatience: glazing eyes, shuffling feet and tapping pencils are all sure indicators of loss of audience interest. Nor, unless you are really confident of your ability to amuse, should you rely too heavily upon a humorous story to capture the audience's attention or to break the ice. It takes only a small error of timing, a moment's forgetfulness at a critical point, to cause such a story to fall completely flat—leaving you facing a stony-faced audience which may be wondering whether your delivery of the remainder of your presentation will be equally gauche. To summarize: get to the point quickly; use clear, concrete language; avoid generalities; and be brisk and businesslike, not hesitant and laborious.

Step 2. State what is wrong with the present situation. In my own experience of listening to presentations by training officers, neglect of this step is unquestionably the biggest single cause of their subsequent failure to convince and persuade. All too often I have watched a young enthusiast dash himself to pieces upon a wall of indifference because of his failure to undermine his audience's confidence in their present methods or practices. And yet, surely, it

126

is the height of *naïveté* to expect any man to be motivated to take action upon a problem which, for him, does not exist? No rational human being, in a situation which affects his livelihood, will willingly accept a proposal which may smack of change for the sake of change, with all its attendant discomforts and uncertainties. Who can blame him for clinging to the comfortable certitudes of the traditional ways?

Whether he uses a scalpel or a spade to achieve his purpose the training officer must ruthlessly dissect the attitudes, methods or practices which he is seeking to change. He must point to the price which is being paid, either in human or material terms (or both) for their continued existence; he must present his audience with well-marshalled facts and figures which support his argument; above all, he must demonstrate his knowledge and understanding of the problems which confront his audience. In short, he must identify with their problems—not adopt 'know-all' or 'holier-than-thou' attitudes which will quickly brand him as a bumptious young theorist.

All this means that his research before the meeting must be thorough and systematic. Facts must be verified, figures checked and rechecked and examples carefully selected for their relevance to the current situation. By his diligence in preparing this section of his case, the training officer can ensure not only the respect and confidence of his audience but also their willingness to listen to his proposed solution. And unless he can create such a climate, he will be wasting his time.

Step 3. State what must be done to remedy the situation. By the time you have finished step 2, no one at the meeting should have the slightest doubt that a real problem exists and that it merits prompt attention. The stage is now set for you to present your solution. But before you unveil your principal recommendations, it frequently pays dividends to analyse briefly the various other alternatives which you considered, giving in each case your reasons for discarding them. Such tactics tend to generate confidence in your judgement by providing further evidence of the depth and quality of your thinking. An additional advantage is that you can often spike a potential critic's guns.

Needless to say, your presentation of your solution must be a model of clarity: any obscurity at this stage will be utterly disastrous. Your audience needs to understand clearly not only the mechanics of your proposal—the hows, wheres and whens—but also *who* will be accountable for achieving results. Above all, there must be no doubt whatever about the relevance of your recommendations to the weaknesses and shortcomings which you exposed during step 2: it was these, after all, which you used to trigger their interest. Do not forget also to acknowledge any help or advice which some members of the group may have given you in your preparatory work—many people resent their ideas being used without due recognition or, in some cases, without their specific agreement.

If you decide to use visual aids, to illustrate certain aspects of your proposal, make sure that they are legible from every quarter of the room. Nothing irritates an audience more than minute lettering and symbols which can barely be deciphered even by those who are most favourably placed to see. Remember, too, that any handouts which you may distribute during your presentation will instantly compete with you for the audience's attention. Unless, therefore, you intend them to be studied immediately as an integral part of your presentation, it is better to distribute them at the end of your talk so that they can be scrutinized during the time set aside for questions and discussion.

You cannot hope to anticipate every possible question which you may be asked during the discussion of your presentation. Nevertheless, if your thinking and research have been thorough and systematic, you will undoubtedly be aware of at least *some* of the major issues which would arise if your proposal were to be accepted. It is these known and predictable problems of implementation which you can often dispose of during this stage of your presentation—with impressive consequences for your prestige with the audience. Such tactics, however, require considerable self-discipline since too great an emphasis upon potential problems may lead some of your more timid listeners to conclude that your remedy will cause more problems than it will cure.

Step 4. State the cost of your proposal. Some ideas cost virtually nothing to implement: they require only a change of attitude or a reallocation of existing resources. Since the essence of a good business decision is that it secures maximum benefits at the lowest possible cost, it follows that a proposal which involves only a very modest financial outlay—or even no outlay at all—has a built-in advantage over one which would be more costly to implement. Incredibly enough, some training officers seem to be totally unaware of the importance of this point when presenting such proposals, thus failing to exploit one of their most powerful assets.

More often, however, change involves expense and such costs must, of course, be justified. Nevertheless, at this stage in your presentation, your principal aim should be to ensure that the audience clearly understands the total cost of the items which may be required, especially where running costs are involved in addition to the capital outlay. For example, let us suppose that you were advocating the purchase of an overhead projector for use during internal company training courses. Clearly, the total expense involved would include not merely the cost of the projector itself: it would also have to cover the cost of a transparency maker, a screen and supplies of transparencies.

Failure to present cost information clearly and comprehensively is the Achilles heel of many presentations by training officers. Except in cases where only a few basic items are involved, it is better to present such material either in the form of a classified handout or by using well-designed visual aids. In all cases, it is vital at this stage for the speaker to slow down the speed of his delivery to allow time for the figures to be absorbed by the audience.

128

Hasty and rapid delivery of financial or technical data can easily ruin an otherwise competent presentation.

Step 5. State the advantages—and make a positive ending. This is your final opportunity to motivate the audience to react favourably to your proposal—make the most of it!

Never say that the advantages of your scheme are obvious: they may be obvious to *you* but you have no right to assume that they are equally clear to the audience. It is your job to drive home the advantages of your proposal—do not rely upon the group to do this work for you.

Like the effective salesman who is trying to persuade a potential customer to purchase his product, you must talk benefit language. This means that you must spell out the advantages of your proposal, clearly and specifically, showing how the members of the group would benefit, either individually or collectively. Remember, too, that an audience is far more likely to be impressed by quantitative evidence than by vague generalizations. It is much more effective to be able to state that your proposal will save x man-hours per day, month or year than merely to say that it will save time and labour.

Try to end your talk on a confident, optimistic note. To sit down abruptly with a muttered 'that's all I have to say' is a very limp way of concluding a presentation. Sometimes a well-known quotation may be appropriate as an ending, or perhaps a reference can be made to some aspect of the company's performance in which everyone takes pride. The essential point is that you should avoid ending 'not with a bang but a whimper'. Most people tend to remember a speaker's final remarks much more clearly than his earlier comments and it is vital that you leave them with a favourable impression.

Conclusion

In this chapter I have outlined a systematic method of presenting a proposal for change to a group of people within an organization. The plan can be modified for situations involving only a few people or even for a meeting with a single individual. While it is based upon a logical sequence of questions and answers, it should be used flexibly and not as a rigid formula—there is ample scope for the trainer to exercise his personal judgement and initiative.

The really important point for the training officer to recognize is that his professional expertise needs to be sold if it is to make an impact upon his customers. This, in turn, requires him to attain a high level of competence in his personal selling skills: knowledge, like patriotism, is not enough.

As with other types of change agent in industry today, training men succeed or fail according to their ability to communicate. Whether we welcome it or resent it, we are all salesmen now.

23

How to identify potential managers

Selecting the right people for jobs in first-line management, whether in sales or in any other area, is one of the most important and difficult decisions that management has to take. The costs of selecting the wrong man are notoriously high both to the company and to the man himself—as well as to those people who report to him. Invariably, in any company with poor supervision there is poor morale, reflected in such unwelcome phenomena as high staff turnover, constant bickering and in-fighting between individuals, sluggish performance and indifferent results.

The problem is particularly acute in the case of first-level supervisory appointments because all too often there is a complete lack of 'hard' evidence regarding the candidate's managerial potential. A manager who is being considered for a more senior job can at least be partially measured on his 'track record'—his previous and current performance as a manager—but in the case of first-line appointments no such record exists. As a result, the selection decision frequently becomes little more than an act of faith, based on hunch and hearsay rather than on objective data.

Let us take a familiar example. John Smith, a young dynamic salesman, is considered a strong candidate for promotion to sales supervisor. For three consecutive years he has exceeded his quotas, controlled his costs and opened many profitable new accounts. He is articulate, enthusiastic, sociable and highly presentable. At first sight he would seem to have excellent potential for further advancement. But is this really so? Surely our information about his ability to cope with a management job is still sadly incomplete? For example:

1. What is known about his ability to lead other people? How is he likely to handle the problems of man-management?
2. What motivates him and how does he think others are motivated? What kind of management style does he favour? How acceptable will he be to the people he will be leading?

3. How clever is he? What kind of mental firepower does he have? What is his level of reasoning ability? Can he think clearly?
4. How well does he communicate? How is he likely to shape up at meetings? Can he influence people in a group environment as opposed to selling to a customer in an informal face-to-face situation?

Since the manager usually has no real answer to these questions he is forced to use his best judgement on the evidence available, much of which may be hearsay rather than the result of direct personal experience of the man. And so, stifling any nagging reservations he may have, he promotes Smith and hopes for the best.

But instead of using this 'faith, hope and charity' approach, should he not have attempted to reduce the element of risk by trying to obtain answers to at least some of these questions *before* he appointed Smith? Perhaps he might still have taken the wrong decision—no selection system is infallible—but the chances of his doing so would have been considerably reduced since he would have possessed information directly related to Smith's *managerial potential* rather than to his record as a salesman. In short, he would have been able to predict the probability of Smith's success or failure with far greater confidence.

Fine words, but how can this be done? Surely only by observing the man *in action* in a series of exercises designed to provide objective evidence of his management potential? Contrived as this approach may seem, it represents a considerable advance on some of the more traditional methods, such as the individual interview, which have so often proved depressingly inexact as predictors of success. After all, the fact that a man shines (or, for that matter, fails to shine) in an interview situation tells you nothing about his ability to get along with other people—still less about his powers of leadership or his true level of intelligence. You can only hope to obtain evidence of the 'whole man' by exposing him to a situation in which he will be required to compete with men of similar background and experience in performing tasks relevant to the management job.

But which tasks *are* most relevant to the job of the sales supervisor? And among the hundred-and-one talents it would be desirable for him to have, which stand out as being exceptionally critical? Surely there are three which are pre-eminent: first, the ability to lead, motivate and inspire a predominantly extrovert working group; second, the ability to communicate effectively both within the organization and with customers; and third, skill in handling the kind of human problems that arise, often in a very dramatic way, as a result of leading men who operate in an aggressive external environment. Clearly, while such a man will not need to have a stratospheric IQ, he will certainly need a good measure of mental agility and resilience—in the practical sense of being able to think clearly and quickly and to come up with solutions to problems in situations where time is short and resources are often inadequate. We are looking, then, for a mature, self-confident man whose need for self-fulfilment is satisfied primarily through successful competition with his environment and the people within it.

So much for theory. How can these concepts be applied in practice? The remainder of this chapter will attempt to answer this question, using experience recently gained within a large divisional sales force of 3M U K.

Background

Operating over a wide range of industrial and consumer markets, the sales force—120 strong—had generated considerable product growth throughout 1972 and 1973. It was clear that if the division were to grasp its opportunities in an ever-growing market, its management structure would have to be radically reorganized and strengthened, necessitating the creation of a number of regional sales supervisor posts in various parts of the UK.

It was vitally important that the right man should be selected for these posts and, since company policy is to promote wherever possible from within, it was decided to subject the potential candidates from the sales force to a far more searching scrutiny than had been traditional in the past. Instead of simply continuing to select from a small coterie of star salesmen, management determined that all salesmen with more than one year's service should attend a series of one-day assessment programmes which would give each individual an opportunity to demonstrate both his management potential and his particular needs for further training and development.

Using one year's service as an entry qualification had two major advantages. First, since nearly 70 per cent of the sales force was eligible to attend, it eliminated any lurking suspicions that the programmes were intended only for 'crown princes'. Secondly, it gave management the opportunity to take stock of a far larger group of potential candidates than would have been possible under the old regime. This proved to be a vital factor in enlisting support for the programme since it was clearly in the interest of every sales manager to have a wider selection of candidates to choose from.

The structure of the programme

Groups of salesmen, drawn from a wide variety of product groups within the division, were assembled for one-day assessment programmes at approximately fortnightly intervals throughout the period September–December 1973. Each group consisted of nine men and their performance on the various practical exercises was observed and assessed by a team of three senior managers—two from the division and one from the corporate training department. While the training manager remained a constant fixture on all the programmes, fresh teams of divisional assessors were used on each occasion so that by the end of the project all senior sales managers had gained experience of the relevant assessment techniques.

Since it was considered unrealistic to expect every assessor to appraise all nine salesmen in detail, each was allocated a group of three individuals to review in depth—a policy which ensured that all members of the group received specialized attention. Moreover, no assessor was ever allocated a salesman from his own product team. This, of course, added very considerably to the impartiality and objectivity of the assessment process since it meant that assessors were always appraising men who were strangers to them and about whom they had no preconceived ideas.

The exercises

1. **Leadership.** Each programme began with a 45-minute group discussion on a general topic to which any salesman could reasonably be expected to contribute. For example, one of the most frequently-discussed questions was 'In how many ways can salesmen be motivated and which are the most important factors—and why?' The discussions were completely unstructured, i.e., no formal leader was appointed by the assessors, this being a decision which was left to the group members themselves (in fact, only two of the nine groups chose to appoint a chairman).

The assessors' task was to monitor the members' contributions for evidence of leadership ability which, for the purpose of the exercise, was defined as 'the ability to communicate, interpret and defend an opinion in such a way that it was generally accepted by the group'. Those who did well tended to be mature, self-confident men who could both give and take criticism without upsetting others or becoming over-emotional themselves. The assessment form which was used to rate each individual's contribution is shown in Fig. 23.1.

2. **Skill in communication.** As in many other marketing-oriented organizations, the company's sales supervisors are frequently called upon to make formal presentations both at in-company meetings and at external gatherings where existing or potential customers are present. Skill in effective speaking is therefore a major requirement of the job.

Each salesman was therefore given 15 minutes to prepare a 10-minute presentation for delivery to the other members of the group. Sometimes members were given complete freedom to choose their own subjects; on other occasions they were each given a choice of three (a current affairs topic, a recreational subject and one concerned with some aspect of selling). Evidence of good preparation and organization of material was looked for, in addition to competence in delivery, and once again the observers were provided with some assessment guidelines (see Fig. 23.2).

Fig. 23.1   Guidelines for assessors: group discussion

Which of the following ratings, in your view, comes closest to reflecting the individual's performance? N.B. If you wish, you may use + or − signs to indicate degrees of performance within each rating.

A. An outstanding contributor. Consistently contributed ideas which were relevant, logical and clearly expressed. Showed marked ability to influence the group in a positive manner and was clearly respected by his colleagues.

B. A good contributor. Introduced some valuable ideas and expressed them clearly. Well respected by the group without being regarded as its natural leader.

C. A satisfactory contributor. Occasionally contributed his own ideas but more often followed up or commented upon someone else's ideas. Made only a moderate impact upon the group.

D. A poor contributor. Most of his contributions were irrelevant and badly expressed. Made little impact upon the group.

E. A very poor contributor. Such contributions as he made were trivial and very badly expressed. Played no constructive part in the discussion.

Fig. 23.2   Guidelines for assessors: individual presentations

1. Introduction:	Did he state his subject clearly?
2. Material:	Was his material well organized?
3. Word choice:	Did he use clear, straightforward language?
4. Audience contact:	Did he look at the audience?
5. Audibility:	Could he be heard easily?
6. Variety of tone:	Was his voice interesting to listen to?
7. Speed of delivery:	Did he speak at a comfortable pace?
8. Mannerisms:	Were you distracted by any verbal or physical mannerisms?
9. Conclusion:	Did he 'round off' his talk competently?
10. Conviction:	Did he convey sincerity/enthusiasm?

3. **Management style.** The exercise chosen was a deceptively innocuous-looking case study (The Joe Bailey Action Maze) involving a problem of persistent absenteeism on the part of an employee with a previously unblemished conduct record—a man, moreover, who was regarded as one of the most productive members of his working group.

Each member was given a brief statement of the problem and invited to make a decision from a list of six possible courses of action. Depending upon his choice, he then received another sheet informing him of the results of his action and requesting him to deal with the new situation by selecting another decision from a further set of six alternatives. This pattern was repeated for about 45 minutes, involving an average of 20 decisions by each participant, and by analysing the decisions made it proved possible to detect each individual's 'preferred' management style, i.e., the one he would be most likely to use when dealing with real-life human relations problems.

4. Reasoning ability. The test used was the well-known AH6 Reasoning Test (available in the UK from the National Foundation for Educational Research) which was administered by the sales employment manager who had previously been trained and licensed to use it. This one-hour test consists of 60 questions of which 50 per cent measure verbal reasoning ability, the remainder being equally divided between numerical and diagrammatic problems.

University graduate 'norms' were applied to the test scores to obtain the individual ratings since it was felt desirable that future sales managers should possess a level of reasoning ability associated with advanced educational achievement, even though only a few of the salesmen tested held college degrees.

Predictably, the results of this test discriminated much more sharply between high and low performers than those for any of the other three exercises.

The results of the exercises

Most salesmen were much more comfortable with exercises requiring the use of their existing skills as professional communicators and persuaders than with the reasoning test which—especially for some of the older salesmen—contained a considerable element of 'cultural shock'. Many of those in the 40+ age group had never before taken any kind of 'paper and pencil' test, unlike some of the younger men who had become acclimatized to such exercises during their formal education.

However, even in the more familiar territory of speech-making and discussion there were marked inconsistencies in many of the individual performances. Some salesmen who had shone in the general discussion gave only mediocre presentations and vice versa; others who had done well as communicators proved to be naïvely autocratic in their handling of the human relations problem; while among the relatively small group who 'passed' the reasoning test there were several who did poorly on one or more of the other three exercises.

Such variations were, of course, entirely to be expected. Indeed, it would have been astonishing if they had not occurred during a process which, after all, was seeking evidence of four different kinds of ability. It is precisely such elements of inconsistency—irrationality even—in human performance which constitute the perennial challenge of the manager's job.

Evaluation and summary

While it is still too early to claim any spectacular success for this approach to identifying potential sales managers, the performance of the dozen or so men who have been promoted since attending the programmes has encouraged the company to extend the new procedures to a further 200 salesmen operating in three of its largest product groups.

There are, potentially, five major benefits sales management can confidently expect to reap from a well designed and competently administered assessment programme:

1. The opportunity to observe potential promotion candidates in competitive interaction with their peers. No selection interview can provide this kind of data.
2. The opportunity to obtain evidence of a wider range of abilities than it is possible to detect at the conventional interview—for example, leadership, creativity and inter-personal skills.
3. The opportunity to consider the assessments of a number of experienced managers on promotion candidates, based upon evidence of their performance on the programme.
4. The opportunity to devise realistic training and development plans for both groups and individuals, since many training needs are highlighted by the results of the exercises. *This has proved to be a major benefit of the programme within 3M UK.*
5. The opportunity to generate greater salesman confidence in the company's promotion policies by giving all potential candidates the chance to demonstrate their talents. (N.B. During surveys carried out after the project, most salesmen paid tribute to the greater objectivity of a process that gave them the opportunity to show what they could do in a variety of situations—not just in one, such as a selection interview.)

Some limitations

It would be naïve to pretend that any selection process can provide management with an infallible tool for predicting human performance. There is nothing automatic about either success or failure and sometimes even the most confident predictions can be confounded. Managers should recognize that the programmes described are not magical procedures which completely eliminate the possibility of errors occurring in selection situations. They in no way diminish the selector's need to exercise his judgement. But they do provide him with better and more rounded information upon which to base his decisions.

Secondly, it has to be conceded that this type of programme does tend to favour those who are by nature more confident, articulate and extrovert. The shy man who is reluctant to contribute will be at a distinct disadvantage unless he is prepared to discard his inhibitions and participate enthusiastically. On the other hand, one might reasonably argue that such a man would be unlikely to succeed in sales management anyway.

136

Finally, it must never be forgotten that his attendance at such a programme represents only one day's activity, one day's performance, in a man's life. In order to make a balanced judgement in a future promotion situation, *it is essential that all other relevant sources of information about his performance and personality are utilized and considered.* This does *not* mean listening to hearsay or gossip: it *does* involve a systematic search for more hard facts about the man which can be weighed in the balance with the evidence obtained from his performance on the programme.

Conclusion

There are few elements more destructive of an organization's morale than widespread employee cynicism about promotion procedures. Justice must be *seen* to be done. The programme which has been described is simply another staging post on that long and arduous journey many companies are now making towards a more open business society—perhaps the only kind that can survive in the turbulent years ahead.

24

How to revitalize
a tired trainer

Running training courses is an exacting job. In essence, the trainer must live by his wits—by the relevance of his material, the skill of his presentation and the power of his personality. Like an actor, he is always 'on stage' and news of his successes and failures carries far beyond the conference room, eventually establishing him—for better or worse—as a public figure within his company. Not surprisingly, in view of the extrovert nature of his role, the trainer is subject to many psychological strains and pressures which at times can result in a marked deterioration in his performance.

Trainers who deal with a narrow rather than a wide range of courses are especially liable to 'run out of steam'. It takes enormous reserves of enthusiasm and dedication to keep on running successfully a course which one may have run a hundred or more times before. Often a kind of 'battle fatigue' sets in which, if unchecked, can easily result in the trainer transmitting his feelings of boredom and lassitude to the group itself. When this happens, the outcome can be, and often is, disastrous, since men cannot be expected to learn from a trainer who is lacking in enthusiasm and panache. The effect which a bored trainer can have on a company over a period of time is thus obvious.

This problem is one to which no facile answers can be given, since every trainer has his own unique blend of strengths and weaknesses. Nevertheless, improvement is unlikely to occur by chance, so there is a need for a systematic approach—one which can be readily adapted to the requirements of the individual. This chapter will deal with such an approach, using a real-life case history to illustrate how the principles can be applied.

Step 1: Analyse performance. Eric Smith (as we shall call him) was a sales training officer, responsible for the initial training of all new salesmen in the consumer products group of a major company. Aged 38, he had been in his job for about five years. He ran only one course—a 10-day basic training course, the content of which was equally divided between product knowledge and selling skills. Since salesman turnover was high, he often ran

138

the course for several months at a time, with occasional short breaks for field training and visits to the regional sales offices.

Shortly after the company had appointed a corporate training adviser to coordinate training at all levels throughout the organization, the latter was requested by Eric's superior, the general sales manager (GSM), to devise a refresher training programme which would check the alarming deterioration in Eric's performance. The training adviser arranged to 'sit in' as an observer on several sessions of the standard course, as a result of which he drew up the 'balance sheet' shown in Fig. 24.1.

Step 2: Devise improvement plan. The balance sheet was then discussed by the training adviser at a meeting with both Eric and the GSM. Far from resenting criticism, Eric expressed strong appreciation of the efforts being made to improve his performance which he was conscious had not been meeting his former high standards. As a result of this discussion, an action programme was agreed, the objectives being:

1. To improve the effectiveness of the present course for newly-appointed salesmen.
2. To challenge Eric's ability to 'grow' in his job, i.e., to provide him with opportunities to improve his knowledge and skills.

Step 3: Implement improvement plan. The plan was divided into four main phases, each of which is now discussed.

Phase A: refresher training
Eric was sent on a short external course for sales training specialists, following a searching investigation by the training adviser into the content of the course and the calibre of the instructors. Happily, the course was an unqualified success. Not only did Eric become aware of the many new techniques available in his field: he also took the opportunity of exchanging ideas and experiences with his fellow course members. This, in turn, revitalized his enthusiasm and interest and he returned eager to try out a number of the new ideas and approaches he had discovered.

Two further steps were taken to capitalize on his new found interest. First, he was sent on a two-day 'effective speaking' course to brush up his speaking techniques. Here again, the course had a rejuvenating effect, not least because of the powerful impact made by the use of closed circuit television. Second, the training adviser, having consulted officials of the Institute of Marketing, devised a planned reading programme for him in order to further stimulate his thinking on new training techniques. Thereafter, a monthly meeting was arranged between Eric and the GSM, during which he reported on any relevant new ideas which he has gleaned from his reading and presented his plans for agreement and subsequent implementation.

139

Fig. 24.1 Appraisal of performance of a training officer

Strengths	Needs
1. Good rapport with group members—courteous and patient when dealing with questions.	1. More drive and dynamism in presenting material—lack of enthusiasm and impact.
2. Good knowledge of products.	2. Exposure to new thinking, new techniques (poor use of visual aids).
3. Makes good use of examples drawn from own experience.	3. Better control over group discussion—is easily side-tracked.
	4. A more critical, challenging approach to course members' comments and opinions.

Summary of Performance Needs

A competent instructor, but needs more drive. Has become somewhat 'stale' as a sales trainer and needs to recapture his enthusiasm by developing a more analytical and creative approach to his job, coupled with a more dynamic and challenging presentation of his material.

Phase B: critical analysis of present course

It was clear that Eric had become bored with the course that he had been running for so long but that he had made little effort to improve it. Now that his enthusiasm had returned, the time was ripe for a 'job enrichment' exercise in which he himself would play a major role.

He was requested by the GSM to carry out a rigorous critique of the existing course—to put each and every element, as it were, 'on trial for its life'. As mentioned earlier, Eric had already formed a number of new ideas as a result of his refresher course and planned reading programme. He now spent two weeks, both at head office and in the sales regions, intensively discussing the effectiveness of the standard course with sales managers and supervisors and, not least, with many of his former 'pupils' who were operating in the field. During this exercise, he amassed a great deal of data which enabled him to identify those areas of salesman performance where improvement was required. He now had a clear understanding of the short-comings of the present course and was fully equipped to begin the necessary restructuring.

Phase C: development of improved course

In the light of the information which he had acquired during the earlier stages of his development programme, Eric now submitted his proposals for improving the course to the GSM and the training adviser. Predictably, there were a number of swingeing changes affecting the content, frequency and duration of the course, as well as the instructional techniques. Even more gratifying, however, was the clear evidence of a basic change in Eric's attitudes towards his job. Whereas previously he had been apathetic and negative in his outlook, he now positively radiated enthusiasm for the changes which he had recommended.

As a final precaution, prior to the introduction of the new course, it was arranged that he would give a 'Preview' presentation at a meeting of group sales managers and supervisors. This took about half a day and, as a result of the suggestions and comments which were made, he was able to make a number of further improvements to the content of the course.

Phase D: introduction and follow-up

The course was duly launched and it was not long before enthusiastic reports began to filter back to the GSM from field sales management. Not only had there been a noticeable improvement in the zest with which the new salesmen were tackling their jobs: the same effects were being observed in some of the older and more experienced salesmen who had attended the course as part of their refresher training. Most important of all, there had been a marked up-swing in business results: the average increase in market penetration during the first six months was of the order of 8 per cent, with only a marginal increase in sales costs. The investment in Eric's development was showing a handsome return.

Nevertheless, it was recognized that it would be easy to lose such gains through complacency and self-admiration. No one saw this more clearly than Eric, who devised a number of searching evaluation procedures which provided him with the necessary feedback to keep his programme up to date.

Step 4: Review and control. Delighted though they were by the improvement in Eric's performance, the GSM and the training adviser recognized that they still had a vital role to play—that of keeping him motivated and healthily critical of his own efforts.

One of Eric's past failings was that he had become too isolated in his head office 'ivory tower' and had lost touch with developments in the field. As a follow-up to his initial development programme, the GSM and the training adviser devised a regular schedule of field visits for him which would ensure frequent contact, not only with field sales management, but also with key account customers and dealer salesmen. Furthermore, at each quarterly meeting of the product management group, he was required to report on any new developments in the marketplace which, in his view, necessitated amendments to his current training programmes. Similarly, ideas and suggestions for improvements were put forward by other members of the group and these were thoroughly investigated, and where practicable, implemented.

As a result of these discussions and his subsequent efforts, Eric soon became accepted as a valuable member of the management team. He is now a strong candidate for a senior sales management post, having recently recruited an assistant whom he is currently developing to take his place in preparation for his own promotion.

Conclusion

No matter how dedicated and enthusiastic a trainer may be, there will be times when his batteries clearly need recharging. For the man who runs a narrow range of courses, with only short intervals between each course, boredom and apathy are ever-present enemies which can quickly undermine his enthusiasm and vitality. At such times, the sympathetic understanding of his boss is vital if his dynamism and self-confidence are to be restored. Given such a framework of support and encouragement, the kind of approach which has been discussed can result in a rapid improvement in personal attitudes and in the subsequent achievement of business objectives.

25

How to win top management support

There are some remarkably *ineffective* strategies for gaining the support of a managing director for training or, indeed, of senior management in general—strategies which, whatever the apparent short-term gains, are bound to end in disaster. These are techniques which should only be used if the trainer is resigned to changing his job every nine to twelve months. The first of these dead-beat strategies to avoid is what might be called the *witch-doctor approach*.

Witch-doctors are employed, among other things, to end droughts, make rain, cure the incurable and sometimes even to try to raise the dead—and some training people allow themselves to be employed in exactly the same way. Just as the witch-doctor festoons himself with leopard's claws and other impressive paraphernalia to ward off evil spirits, so the training man, especially if he is on a behavioural science 'trip', often tends to communicate in a kind of management Swahili which, for sheer wilful obscurity, rivals the small print at the bottom of an insurance policy.

The trainer may rightly be proud of his knowledge of the behavioural sciences and appreciative of the many powerful insights which they have given us into human needs and motivations. But if his conversation is constantly littered with mind-boggling references to 'self-actualization', 'force fields', 'group dynamics', 'synectics', 'psycho-cybernetics', 'interactive skill training', 'transactional analysis', and a host of others, he can hardly complain if his boss begins to regard him as a rather less than able communicator. And if a man cannot communicate with his top management, he is finished.

He must also beware of claiming too much universality, too much certainty, for theories and approaches which, however fascinating they may be and however sincere their advocates, have, in some cases, a somewhat mixed and limited track record. Remember, this is still very new territory: compared with the physical sciences and some of the natural sciences the amount of research undertaken to verify some of these theories has—quite understandably—been extremely small. It ill behoves anybody at this stage to be too dogmatic.

Remember, we always hear about the success stories (often the same ones, over and over again) but rarely hear about the failures and the mountains that have brought forth mice. But there certainly have been failures; and one of the principal causes has been that too much has been hoped for, too much promised, too much sold and too little delivered. People can be cussed, unpredictable, illogical and emotional just as often and just as easily as they can be mature, cooperative, rational and self-disciplined. Maybe some of the behavioural science messiahs could use a little more humility before they indulge in global generalizations about human behaviour: and maybe training people could sometimes use a little more restraint and common sense in the way they sell their ideas to colleagues in line management.

A second danger is *credit-snatching*. The training manager must keep a sense of proportion about the kind of contribution which training can realistically be expected to make, recognizing its limitations as well as its strengths. After all, the sales force may be the best-trained in its industry: but if the product is dying, its pricing is wrong and the marketing strategies are blatantly senile, then the salesmen, however excellent their training, are going to have a very hard time. Certainly, if things are going well—and continue to go well consistently, year in, year out, those responsible for training can reasonably assume that they are making a valid contribution to the success of the business. But theirs is only one component, one contribution: many others are in there pitching, too. If the drum is beaten too boldly in good times, the beater must also expect to carry the can in bad times. And line management will take considerable pleasure in seeing that he does.

Third, however flattering it may be to the ego—and there's nothing wrong with a trainer having a well-developed ego (he certainly needs a thick skin)—the temptation to assume the role of a potent adviser, the power behind the throne, must be resisted. There is an awful precedent in Rasputin, the so-called 'mad monk' of Tsarist times, who united a jealous nobility against him and suffered a dreadful fate because of his lethal capacity to bite off more than he could chew. The trainer should take care to see that his advice is within his area of competence and should not pontificate upon, or appear to be trying to take over, responsibilities which rightly belong to others. He should ensure, for example, that his managing director really understands that training is essentially a *line management responsibility* and influence him to see that line managers carry out their responsibilities for developing their people in their day-to-day management of the job. After all, this is where the *real development* takes place—not simply in the classroom, which is an artificial environment at the best of times and can rarely reproduce the urgency, the pressures and the challenges which are experienced on the job itself.

Line management's commitment to training can be built into a performance appraisal system—by requiring an appraiser to record on the appraisal form what, in his view, are the man's priority training needs. Having done that, the obvious question can be popped—what specific action do you personally intend to take to develop him or to remedy his shortcomings? And he can be

144

required to *write down* his plan on the appraisal form. The man himself can be committed to accept, where relevant, depending upon his needs, a measure of responsibility for *developing himself*. It might be through attending a course of evening classes or by taking a correspondence course or by undertaking a planned reading programme which will broaden his perspective and enable him to profit by the experience of others.

Only after the boss and the subordinate have considered what they can do to bring about an improvement should they be expected (if it is necessary) to call in the management training specialist. It is wrong to wet-nurse people by using the training man as a kind of all-purpose nanny. Managers should be as self-motivated in the training area as in any other area: and you will not get that kind of commitment if they are encouraged to call in the trainer as a kind of reflex action, instead of first thinking through the situation for themselves.

But even this is not enough. After all, talk is cheap and there has never been a shortage of platitudes in the management development business. To show people that games are not being played, two things are necessary. First, a written policy because this constitutes an authority for, and a commitment to, action. Second, the introduction of some mechanisms to bring about the kind of action which is needed. To take the policy point first: 3M has a simple but comprehensive policy statement on management development. Two items from that statement demonstrate that the company does not 'play games'— that, in fact, it means what it says on training: 1. 'Every manager will plan, organize and delegate to allow himself sufficient time to (a) participate in activities planned to further his own development and (b) assist in the development of his immediate subordinates.'

This reminds managers, quite unequivocally, that they are responsible both for developing themselves and for providing appropriate development opportunities for their staff. And it also reminds them that they have a duty to *make time* for these activities by effective planning and delegation. As Peter Drucker once said 'there is no shortage of time: there is only a lack of priorities'.

From the Ten Commandments downwards, all policy statements have been bedevilled by problems of enforcement (not the most popular of words in these democratic days). Nevertheless, a policy which has teeth—and which is integrated with the system of rewards and punishment under which managers work—has an infinitely better chance of being implemented than one which, however majestically phrased, is little more than a paper tiger. Here the second policy item comes in. 2. 'The achievement of effective results in the development of his immediate subordinates will be an important factor in the appraisal of a manager's performance.' (The 'effective results' referred to, include, of course, encouraging the subordinate to develop himself.) The next logical step is to integrate these concepts into that traditional management tool for auditing management performance—the annual performance appraisal.

145

If the trainer should avoid being a witch-doctor, a credit-snatcher or an *eminence grise,* then what *should* he try to be—that is, if he wants to survive the next major downward swing in the business cycle? The answer, for once, is simple: *he has to think, act and project like a businessman.* He has to find out what the market needs and supply it; and he has to find out what it is going to need and *get ready* to supply it. In other words, he has to be customer-oriented, like the good salesman he needs to be, not product-oriented, trying to force unwanted castor oil down unwilling throats.

Carrying out a really thorough market survey (or a training needs analysis) is a time-consuming chore, and the bigger the company the bigger the chore. Unfortunately, there is no real alternative, because this is the only way to get the facts which are needed to build a credible programme—one which meets the real needs of the business. It is easy, especially for a trainer who is new to a company, to assume that he has seen it all before and that what worked in Company A will work in Company B—neglecting the fact that the people are different, the culture and traditions are different, the market strategies are different, the management style is different and invariably the politics are different, too.

That extra bit of custom tailoring can make all the difference between success and failure. Gaining the respect of professionals means that trainers have to be professionals themselves. And that means researching, digging, discussing and, above all, *listening.* If you stop listening to others, whoever they may be, then you stop learning, and no one is more vulnerable in a company than an obsolete trainer.

Many American businessmen are not particularly accustomed to a research-based, needs-based approach: they are more used to a packaged approach to training—the 'convenience foods' approach—as exemplified by such well-known packages as Kepner-Tregoe and the Blake Grid. These packages can do an excellent job, when sensibly slotted into an overall training strategy. But the basic components and design of that strategy must be the trainer's, the tactics must be his, and, above all, *he* must decide the timing of his various training projects.

Many a trainer has come into a company firing from the hip and spraying a bewildered management with sophisticated theories and packages which have proved completely irrelevant to that company's needs. It's better to start with something which managers recognize that they need rather than with something which they have to be persuaded that they need. They will be far more ready to give a trainer the benefit of the doubt later on, when he is trying to sell something new and radical, if in the past he has delivered the goods which were specifically asked for.

The use of the managing director's time is crucial. It must be time used responsibly—he is a great deal more valuable to the company than any trainer because he makes bigger decisions which commit far greater resources. He cannot be expected always to go out front selling training ideas and lustily clobbering any of his senior colleagues who may be less than enthusiastic. He has to live with his colleagues, and if he enjoys a great deal of freedom himself he should be reluctant to impinge upon the freedom of others—and freedom includes the right to disagree and to remain unconvinced. It is the trainer's job to convince these people.

The managing director, or indeed any other senior manager, is interested in benefits and results, not in theory. He cannot be expected to keep on genuflecting to somebody else's personal gods when his primary interest is in running a profitable business—and in seeing that it stays that way. He will not be impressed by endless recitals of wondrous deeds performed in far-away places by people with strange-sounding names, but he certainly *will* be interested in what is proposed to make his own organization more effective. He needs to be shown what needs and problems the trainer has uncovered and to discuss the effect which they are having on the business.

The trainer should pile on the agony. Emphasize the loss, the waste, the turnover, the frustration which will result—indeed are happening now—if no action is taken. Excite his superior's interest with skilfully deployed facts, figures and examples: after all, you cannot expect a man to be motivated to take action on a problem unless he realizes just how serious that problem is. When—and only when—the trainer has got his interest should he present his boss with a solution and spell out the benefits loud and clear. You cannot, of course, always quantify and measure the results which are expected; naturally, any trainer who can is off to a flying start. If he is seeking to change attitudes, for example, he is operating in much more difficult terrain, and it will probably take a long time for the new concepts to become fully absorbed into management's bloodstream: and for evidence of this to become apparent.

When you try to change a man's attitude you are competing with (and often against) the influences of heredity, home environment, education, social class, work experience, company traditions, company politics and sometimes, if operating as an expatriate, national cultural traditions too. These are all powerful factors and they do not disappear overnight—and nobody should be allowed to go away believing that they will. A managing director is perfectly capable of understanding that this is a long-term process—after all, he makes more long-range decisions than anyone else in the company and he knows only too well how long some of them take to pay off. But he will not easily forgive a man whom he thinks has conned him into buying a product with a delivery date which turns out later to have been pure fantasy. And who can blame him?

A trainer cannot expect to keep on having top level, global type discussions with the managing director—and, frankly, he should not need to do so if he is the kind of self-motivated man who prefers to get on with the job. Nevertheless, the MD does need to be kept informed on what's happening so every reasonable opportunity should be taken to get him involved. There is no golden rule here: the strategy must suit the man and the situation. You cannot, for example, expect a man who is by temperament rather shy and reserved to leap to his feet at management meetings and make impassioned orations about the importance of training. He will not do it.

But even managing directors who prefer to keep a fairly low profile do recognize that people expect them, especially on social occasions, to say what are euphemistically termed 'a few well-chosen words'. And provided that they are the right words—and this is a matter of briefing people well in advance—such God-like interventions can often do the cause of training a power of good. Remember, even a whisper from the top at the opening of an important in-company course dinner or cocktail party can sound like a thunderclap two levels further down.

Some training managers like to get their managing directors more deeply involved by inviting them actually to sit in on their courses, but this is rather unkind. If the managing director opens his mouth for very long the chances are that sooner or later he will put his foot in it by saying something which contradicts (or appears to) a key point which the training manager has been battling to get accepted earlier in the course. And the course members will look at their trainer dumbly and accusingly like stricken oxen. If on the other hand he stays tactfully silent—and this is a challenge of historic dimensions for some managing directors—then course members, not knowing which way the cookie is going to crumble, are likely to conclude that silence is golden and give a creditable imitation of the inmates of a Trappist monastery. Either way the course loses.

There are easier and more subtle ways of getting the message across. Sometimes, for example, it may be obvious that there are certain individuals in the company—not necessarily always at board level—in whom the managing director has much confidence and trust; often people whom he has known since they first joined the company together. Concentrating missionary zeal upon these people can often turn them into extremely useful salesmen of new ideas—and these salesmen have no credibility problems and have no difficulty in gaining access to the inner sanctum.

Of course, there are occasions when the direct involvement of the managing director can be of enormous value, especially when a major change in some aspect of a company's philosophy and practice is sought. For example, if the issues are highly-charged politically within the company, the trainer may decide to use the good old 'Trojan Horse' technique and get an outside speaker (or a series of outside speakers) to, as it were 'soften up' the internal opposition. Naturally, if this is to have any chance of succeeding, he needs to select a speaker who is right for the company and to brief him meticulously: he also needs to obtain the support of the managing director. And once again this is going to involve some skilful selling, using the benefits-centred approach mentioned earlier.

Given success at this stage, the next desirable move is to arrange for the managing director to meet the speaker, partly so that the boss can satisfy himself that the man is of the right calibre and is likely to make the right kind of impact. Again, assuming that things go smoothly, it becomes the most natural thing in the world to invite the managing director to introduce the speaker and to chair the meeting. And if the ground is properly prepared—which means properly (with no short-cuts)—the chances are that he will jump at the opportunity, providing the best of all possible starts. After that the trainer is on his own. As a good professional, he should have a well-planned follow-up strategy ready and waiting to exploit the beach-head which the managing director has helped to win.

External courses and conferences can sometimes be used to assist in this seed-planting process; but, again, the trainer has to be realistic. Most M D's are cagey about attending courses, and no wonder—they are usually fantastically busy people, and they have a business to run. They also tend to worry about the kind of people whom they are likely to meet on the course—whether they will be of the same calibre, maturity and experience as themselves or, horror of horrors, whether the course director himself will turn out to be a man incapable of running that proverbial sweet shop.

The package merchants, of course, shrewd marketeers that they are, cater for these factors by running abbreviated versions of their standard courses under enticing labels in which the magic words 'director', 'executive' or even 'presidential' frequently appear. They are simply using a sound psychological approach to this particular sector of the market. Indeed, if a course lacks this kind of elitist appeal for the top manager, the trainer will almost certainly be in for an uphill battle.

At the end of the day—and sometimes it can be a very long day—he is going to be judged not for what he knows but by what he has accomplished. Like any other key specialist what he is being paid for basically is his *judgement* and the quality of his advice. Technical knowledge—knowledge of current theory and practice in the field—is largely taken for granted. What has to be proved continuously is that the trainer can diagnose a problem correctly, recognize where the priorities lie and devise solutions which are relevant and practicable. Personnel and training people have many in-built advantages over other staff specialists. They operate across the whole of the organization, not just a narrow sector of it, they meet people at every level, get to know the problems, the policies, the philosophies, the politics. They should be capable of showing that they have benefited from opportunities and exposure by how they do their jobs.

Trainers often tend to accept too readily, too complacently, that people dislike change. Maybe so. But very often what people really object to and find bewildering is not so much the change itself but the way in which it is presented to them by so-called 'change-agents' who could clearly profit from a little change themselves. So, before words like 'stupid' or 'reactionary' or 'negative' are employed to castigate the unbelievers within companies, a closer look at the training department's own performance as diagnosticians and as salesmen is desirable.

It is very rarely indeed that all the pieces fall gracefully into place just when wanted or expected. Yet to read some of the books and articles on behavioural change, you could be forgiven for thinking that the process of change within companies was a sort of stately, majestic progression, proceeding logically from top to bottom with a certain in-built inevitability about it. It is nothing of the kind. *You get in where you can when you can.*

Appendix 1

Management performance checklist

These notes are intended for use by management training professionals during discussions with managers about their subordinates' training needs. They can also be useful to managers themselves when, for example, they are appraising a man's overall performance or assessing his suitability for promotion.

The questions use the same 'language' as that which we use in our in-company management training programmes. That is to say, they deal with the individual's ability to Plan, Organize, Lead and Control (POLC), and also with such factors as his forcefulness and sincerity, his attitude to conflict and his ability to cope with the emotional pressures of his job. The final questions have to do with his personal qualities—but only to the extent that they affect his performance or are relevant to some other job for which he is being considered.

The checklist is intended to be used simply as an aid and should not be used in a stereotyped fashion. Its purpose is to provide some broad guidelines for discussion and to ensure that all the most important areas of performance are covered systematically.

It covers the following ten main areas:

Planning

1. What is your opinion of his overall planning ability?
2. Is he better at short- or long-term planning?
3. Does he ensure that all the necessary resources are provided?
4. Does he communicate his plans to all who are involved?
5. Does he set realistic deadlines and ensure that they are met?

Organizing

1. Has he established an effective structure for his department or group?
2. Is he alert to the need to make changes when circumstances change?

3. Are his subordinates' responsibilities clearly defined in up-to-date job descriptions?
4. Does he delegate effectively and encourage others to do so?

Leading

1. What is his characteristic method of managing people—for example, is he autocratic or democratic, paternalistic or laisser-faire?
2. Does he consult his subordinates when making decisions?
3. Does he tend to abdicate his authority or is he over-concerned with maintaining it?
4. Does he encourage new ideas or stifle creativity?

Controlling

1. Has he developed effective controls for all major aspects of his operation?
2. Does he ensure that they are implemented?
3. Does he tend to over/under-control?
4. Does he scrap controls which are no longer relevant?
5. Does he develop new controls when they become necessary?

Communicating

1. Does he write clear, concise letters, memoranda and reports?
2. Are his oral presentations well prepared and well delivered?
3. Does he keep you well informed on all significant developments?
4. Does he keep his subordinates well briefed on matters which affect their work?
5. Has he established good communications with other departments?

Problem solving and decision-making

1. Does he tend to over/under-analyse a problem?
2. Is he impetuous/slow to make decisions?
3. Does he tend to pass the buck?
4. Does he anticipate the possible consequences of his decisions and develop good contingency plans?

Training and development

1. Does he constantly try to make the best use of his subordinates' abilities?
2. Does he ensure that they are provided with appropriate training and development opportunities?
3. Does he maintain regular contact with the corporate training department?
4. Does he encourage his people to develop themselves?
5. Has he developed successors for all key posts in his group?

Degree of conviction

1. Can he argue a case logically and persuasively?
2. How does he react to strong criticism?
3. Does he agree too readily with opposing viewpoints?
4. Does he take contrary decisions well?

Innovating

1. Is he constantly looking for better ways of doing his job?
2. Does he encourage his subordinates to be creative?
3. Does he have to be pushed into making changes?
4. Does he discuss new ideas with you before he implements them or does he implement them first and inform you afterwards?

Personal qualities

1. Does he have high standards of personal integrity?
2. Do you trust him and do others trust him?
3. What are his prime motivating factors—money, advancement, recognition, security, the job itself, etc.?
4. How stable is he? Is he likely to stay with the company?
5. How ambitious is he—where does he see his future?
6. How mature is he? Does he take the rough with the smooth or is he easily upset by adverse conditions?

Appendix 2

How to use your graduates: A plea to all executives

From the employer's point of view, the recruitment and training of graduates is a notoriously thankless task. Survey after survey has shown that up to 40 per cent leave their first employers within twelve to eighteen months: cases of a 100 per cent turnover during the first five years are not at all uncommon. As a result of such experiences, some organizations take a totally fatalistic view: the problem is insoluble, therefore we must suffer.

True, the modern graduate is not the most pliable species of industrial recruit. But we cannot have it both ways. If we have selected wisely, we will have purchased curiosity and personality, drive and ambition. Without these qualities, knowledge, by itself, is impotent. Given reasonable good fortune, we may also have acquired men with a zeal for early responsibility and a measure of self-awareness; almost certainly, we shall encounter impetuosity and intolerance. And yet, surely, this irritating amalgam of talent and non-conformity is precisely what a lively company needs—and must obtain. How can one better challenge the smug acceptance of established practice or pierce the intellectual torpor which holds so many in its grip?

'Ah,' say the traditionalists, 'but these new graduates must learn to walk before they can run.' Assuredly, but having taught and encouraged them to walk, can they—the 'old hands'—keep up with them? When confronted by new thinking, by new techniques with outlandish names, do they feel threatened or cheerfully accept that it is high time that *they* began to learn again? Or do they take out insurance against embarrassing creativity by assigning graduates to work which dulls rather than sharpens them so that gradually their enthusiasm wilts and finally expires?

If some firms were to carry out an appraisal of their existing graduate training programmes, they would discover many valid reasons for the present discontent. For example, is the new man *really* expected to benefit from those mind-numbing 'induction courses' which condemn him to long, dreary weeks

154

of 'observing' others at their work? Surely we have not forgotten how it feels to hunger for responsibility, recognition, and an opportunity to achieve?

I believe that we should start with the premise that the young graduate actively desires to use his brains—that he will welcome responsibility and the chance to contribute. What are the implications? One is surely that we ought to desist from deluging him with cataracts of information and, instead, bend our best efforts to unleashing the spirit of inquiry. Why, for example, must he always be *told* by Personnel (with much brandishing of charts) how the company is organized, what are its products and in which markets it earns its daily bread? Could he not be commissioned to find out for himself as part of a 'grass-roots' effort to encourage self-development? In general, we grossly overestimate the time which it takes him to understand established practices— and persistently underestimate his value as critic and innovator.

Of course, there will be times when he will madden his colleagues with his naïvety and tactlessness, and infuriate his superior with his never-ending 'whys?' Occasionally, we shall hear tales of lively confrontations with long-serving stalwarts, of uproar in the typing pool and threatened resignations. Invariably, when taken to task, he will be apologetic and contrite, yet inwardly puzzled—for he has still to learn that, for many human beings, change is unpalatable, and that suggestions for improvements can easily sound like threats. Strong in mental firepower but lacking in subtlety, he will quickly become the target of the corridor commandos, the subject of many a dark look and hostile innuendo. It is at this point that he begins to wonder whether he has chosen the right company—when almost any grass on almost any hill looks greener and more inviting. And so he may decide to leave. Our investment has been wasted.

Yet had we made but a fraction of the effort to keep him that was put into recruiting him, he might have stayed. Did we, for example, ensure that he was given a proper briefing at the time when he joined us? Was he alerted to the fact that success in industry requires not only intellectual power and a lively imagination but also a knowledge of men and an acceptable personality? Was it explained to him that business decisions must of necessity be pragmatic and that there is no such thing as a perfect solution? Was he encouraged to be constructively critical and yet to tread softly and warily when expressing his views? And were these things communicated by the right person—an experienced superior—not by some professional guru from Training Personnel?

As Machiavelli wrote in *The Prince*: 'The first opinion which one forms of a prince, and of his understanding, is by observing the men he has around him.' An executive at any level needs variety in his subordinates—not a team of yes-men or mere carbon copies of himself. In dealing with young graduates, it is better to convince and persuade rather than domineer. Today's young graduate, much more than his predecessor of even five years ago, has a healthy mistrust of corporate paternalism. He looks for evidence of dynamism in thought and action; for a firm company commitment to creativity and growth; and for the opportunity to fulfil himself in a challenging job, under the sympathetic guidance of an enlightened superior.

Appendix 3

Annotated reading list

I am always rather wary of books with voluminous bibliographies—and so, I suspect, are the vast majority of busy, practising managers. I have therefore restricted this reading list to those relatively few authors whose attitudes and ideas are likely to have the greatest impact upon readers whose time is limited.

The following eight books are particularly relevant to the various themes explored in this book:

Adair, J., *Training for Communication*, Macdonald, 1973.
Refreshingly free from jargon and packed with penetrating insights, this book discusses both the principles and practice of good communications with a lightness of touch which is all too rare. Both managers and trainers will find much sound advice on the techniques of effective speaking and running meetings.

Drucker, P. F., *The Practice of Management*, Heinemann, 1955.
Unquestionably the most influential management book of our times and the seed-bed of the modern MbO and 'managerial effectiveness' movements. Reads as freshly and is as relevant as when it was published. The first book to stress that a manager's contribution should be measured by his *results*.

Hague, H., *Executive Self-Development*, Macmillan, 1974.
Demonstrates that managers can only be expected to develop effectively within the context of their jobs and with the active assistance of their immediate superiors. Hague is fiercely critical of the conventional course-centred approach to management development which he regards as time-wasting and ineffectual.

Herzberg, F., *Work and the Nature of Man*, Staples Press, 1968.
This is the definitive statement of Herzberg's theories on motivation which have had such a revolutionary effect upon behavioural science thinking, notably in the field of job enrichment. The book summarizes Herzberg's early findings which gave rise to his theories and quotes later investigations which support his views.

Humble, J. W., *Improving Business Results*, McGraw-Hill, for Management Centre Europe, 1967.

Shows how MbO theories can be translated into effective management practice and that management development must be related to the needs of the business. A tough-minded, pragmatic book which has had a major impact upon the management of progressive companies throughout the world.

Mant, A., *The Experienced Manager*, British Institute of Management, 1969.

A courageous and incisive attack upon the sheer irrelevance of much conventional management training, coupled with a plea for more attention to be devoted to the needs of the older, experienced manager. The effects of Mant's report continue to reverberate around British industry and have led many companies to concentrate upon in-company training and to lessen their dependence upon external courses.

McGregor, D., *The Human Side of Enterprise*, McGraw-Hill, 1960.

As the father of the Theory X and Theory Y concept, McGregor has probably had a greater influence upon modern management thinking than anyone apart from Drucker, and many of the key ideas in modern behavioural science can be traced directly to his pioneer work. In spite of its age, this book has worn remarkably well and, in terms of readability, is still light years ahead of its more recent competitors.

Reddin, W. J., *Effective MbO*, Management Publications, 1971.

Totally practical and immaculately written, this is one of the few really classic books on MbO and is supported by a number of case examples drawn from Reddin's experience as a consultant. Contains a strong critique of conventional job descriptions and emphasizes the importance of focusing upon results, not tasks.

Index

PRINTED AND BOUND IN ENGLAND BY
HAZELL WATSON AND VINEY LTD
AYLESBURY, BUCKS